Learning about magic can sometimes feel a little like reading a cookbook, but *Conjuring Dirt* manages to take an underserved and humble aspect of folk magic and give it new life. Taren acts as a tour guide or museum docent to the world of soils and dirts deployed for sorcerous purposes. This isn't a by-the-numbers sort of tour, though, as Taren enlivens informative sections on graveyard dirt or working at the crossroads with stories drawn from history, folklore, and her own life. You learn about the uses of dirt taken from church grounds or courthouses, but also get the back story on a Beaufort, South Carolina politician who feared that people were hexing him using dirt from a local burnt-down church. She discusses using dirt from an enemy's garden, and takes you to New Orleans and the "Father of the Garden District," whose own botanical bounty was stolen away by his neighbors, piece by piece after his wife died. Like the very best guidebooks or local excursions, you're accompanied by someone who answers your questions before you even ask them and who has a tale to tell, about every stop along the way that makes you feel like you're getting the inside scoop. As a practical guide it's full of useful tidbits, too, but the stories are what will keep you coming back to this compact-but-captivating little book.

Cory Thomas Hutcheson, author of *New World Witchery: A Trove of North American Folk Magic*

Sincere and "down to earth", Taren's *Conjuring Dirt* is an excellent beacon leading us to old and powerful magic that is just beneath our feet. I have worked in the magic of boneyard dirt, gravestone and other dust, purpose, place, and event soil for over 35 years and I attest to its power. The soil is the digested wisdom of everything and everyone that has ever lived. It remembers and holds immense power as the ever-present foundation, garden, dancefloor and pathway for every foot, hoof, fin, belly that has ever walked, slithered, ran or rooted on earth. It is giver of nutrients for all the bodies of life, the final resting place of ancestors, and the accumulative dust of the ancients - dinosaurs, mammoths, redwoods, and humans. Everything we need rests on it, in it, or is composed of it. Could there ever be a more potent and ancient resource for effective conjure and witchery?

Orion Foxwood, traditional witch, southern and Appalachian conjure-man, Faery Seer, and author of *Mountain Conjure and Southern Rootwork*

A fascinating and worthy work. Taren has helped shed new light on a topic too long forgotten underfoot. Sweeping across broad topics and workings Taren still manages to make this book personal and immediate. You will not find here work only for the "professional" or the "expert", although they too will gain from this, no, this book reaches out to not only those just starting out but also those with some experience who are looking to dig deeper. I remain warmed that she took me as a reader not just into the work but also her personal journey, path, and life. She does, in fact, give you dirt on this venerable topic.

Professor Charles Porterfield, author of *Hoodoo Bible Magic*

Conjuring Dirt

Magick of Footprints, Crossroads, &
Graveyards

Conjuring Dirt

Magick of Footprints, Crossroads, & Graveyards

Taren S

**MOON
BOOKS**

Winchester, UK
Washington, USA

JOHN HUNT PUBLISHING

First published by Moon Books, 2023
Moon Books is an imprint of John Hunt Publishing Ltd., No. 3 East Street, Alresford
Hampshire SO24 9EE, UK
office@jhpbooks.net
www.johnhuntpublishing.com
www.moon-books.net

For distributor details and how to order please visit the 'Ordering' section on our website.

ISBN: 978 1 80341 332 7
978 1 80341 333 4 (ebook)
Library of Congress Control Number: 2022941663

A CIP catalogue record for this book is available from the British Library.

Design: Lapiz Digital Services

UK: Printed and bound by CPI Group (UK) Ltd, Croydon, CR0 4YY
Printed in North America by CPI GPS partners

We operate a distinctive and ethical publishing philosophy in all areas of our business, from our global network of authors to production and worldwide distribution.

Contents

Acknowledgements

As I journeyed to many mystical and spiritual places seeking my own sense of self, I gave birth to another magickal being. From the beginning I shielded and at times hid her and our family ties so that she could embrace her own journey and stand separate from me in the magickal community at large.

In the shadows she has stood behind me her entire life. She grew up in the magickal community, quietly making her way, having her own spiritual journey and magickal experiences. In time she came to share space with me and together we founded the *House of Witchcraft*. So much of my world is now hers and this book is a product of that. She is my daughter, and her name is Ashiana S.

To my BFF and secret editor of this book, Robert McCready. Over a decade ago, he walked into Papa Nico's shop with a list of sincere and somewhat amusing questions, and we became friends. He taught me to be proud of my southern heritage, both the good and not so much. In our "sitting on the porch" chats I found the memories and stories that are the foundation of this endeavor. Thank you for the encouragement and extra words when I got lost in a section and giving me a light at the end of the tunnel (so to speak).

To Papa Nico, a Haitian Vodou priest who became my mentor and friend over 30 years ago now. I walked through his shop doors as a young Witch to have many worlds opened to me, forever changing what I thought I knew. He taught humility when I needed it the most. I learned to kneel to understand that I have risen. I will forever be grateful to the universe and forces that be that led me to him.

To the Witches' Cottage Rainbow Coven in San Diego, CA for all the support and encouragement these past five years and counting. They allowed a boomer cisgender to stand center in their space. Amongst them I was gifted with looking upon my world with fresh eyes and new questions. Via their own personal journeys, they taught me to dream bigger than I thought was possible. Their courage is beyond compare in their quest to find their authentic voices. Thank you, I am forever changed for the better. I now understand most of the letters and abbreviations in the community.

To my dearest moonsister, Andrea E. You are irreplaceable, impeccable, and one of a kind. For almost 20 years now you have listened to my stories, some repeatedly and you always lean in and laugh like it was the first time. And much love to that crazy Cajun that for some unknown reason you chose to marry.

To all the magickal practitioners from too many traditions to list that I have shared space with these four decades and counting. Each and every one of you added a piece to the story of me. Thank you so very much.

Foreword

I met Taren in the winter of 2021 during an online magical conference where we both were presenters in our respective fields – me in Rootwork and she in Crossroads Magick. To be clear neither one of us attended the other's presentation; we met in the "meet and greet" virtual room where I was able to share with Taren that I read her book, *Hoodoo in the Psalms,* and my appreciation of the agency she gave to the descendants of African slaves who created Hoodoo. And the rest is history, right? Not quite.

She and I have grown and bonded through space and time since that moment. Regular video chats with both of us being on the opposite sides of the country that could easily last hours or until one of our phones (usually mine) needed charging. Taren has invited me to present, virtually, to her coven or to participate in a conversation with her coven, (which I thoroughly enjoyed) she has interviewed me for her YouTube channel, and a friendship/sisterhood has been and is being cultivated.

Taren asked me if I would be willing to write the foreword to her new book *Conjuring Dirt: Magick of Footprints, Crossroads, and Graveyards.* Of course, I replied with a resounding "Yes!". As a Rootworker, I grow as many of the herbs as possible for use in my work. I never really thought of the dirt as a tool to be used outside of growing things in it. Using dirt was not something I was called to do – then I remembered the mason jar full of red dirt from Georgia that I collected which currently lives on my ancestor altar!

Apparently, my Georgian ancestors wanted to feel their dirt in their space. Yes, this book has shown me various perspectives of using many types of dirt. Now, mind you I was raised in Detroit by a southern-bred mother…dirt was something we kept out of the house and off the front and back porches. Taren has challenged me to view dirt in a special way, after all dirt connects us all.

Dirt leaves behind the energy of the person who stepped in it. Using dirt from footprints creates an opportunity to harm or to bless. That choice is up to the practitioner. Dirt is becoming a more important part of my practice. Knowing that a little goes a long way from gravestone scrapings to even scraping the dirt in between concrete slabs in front of a bank (I live in Detroit – a major city) these collected dirts can go a long way depending on how creative I can be with my rootworking. And I am incredibly creative.

Thanks to Taren's storytelling acumen, she tells her story in a way that made me feel like we are sitting on a veranda in the south, drinking lemonade with sprigs of mint in each glass as she casually tells the story of her life – in part – and anything that would be cautionary would mean an arm grab for inflection. Taren takes you on journey of specific moments in her life where lessons were learned – either good or not so good! In this book are cautionary tales, recipes, proper procedures for collecting dirt, anecdotes, and understanding that no matter where you are, you are standing on dirt and that it is alive with potential.

Taren is NOT a pedantic pontificating writer. Her story flows with lore and worldly examples interspersed in her experiences so the reader sees through her eyes while simultaneously looking around their own sphere and seeing differently the world around them for magical purposes. Her "funky gumbo" makes sense. She gives agency where agency is due.

Taren gives credit to her mentors and is brutally honest about where she comes from and where the magic she uses comes from. She is not an eclectic witch, she is a crossroads witch standing on the dirt and utilizing her knowledge of folk magics, pulling together what is needed, and she challenges the reader to do the same. She challenges the reader to gather what you may need so you have what you will need when you need it, but only if you are called to it. If you did not know before, you will know upon reading this book that Taren's magical practice is her life. It's what she does daily.

Taren's explanation of the crossroads is almost poetic. As a person who stands in the crossroads myself, in order to bridge two worlds, there were times when I needed to sit with something I read and say "Holy smokes, I never thought of it that way!". It is my hope that you, the reader, will uncover new information, apply it to old information and gain a deeper understanding of your dirt and what you can do with it. Go collect your dirt!

Krystal Athena Hubbard
Bridging Worlds Botanica
Detroit, Michigan

Preface

My Dirt

Before you read my words, I need you, the reader, to get a flavor for the dirt that I personally stand upon. What lead me to the point that I am writing this book and why I felt so deeply compelled to do so. My journey to this point is definitely not a straight line unless you count two lefts, a couple of u turns, and a few wrong turns to get to where I stand today.

I am a proud southern conjuring Witch and that is quite a mouth full to say aloud. It took me years to embrace the crossroads I stand upon. My journey to accepting myself, my story, and the land I stand upon was muddled, like any good story.

I grew up in Virginia and North Carolina then migrated to South Carolina and fell in love with the Lowcountry area. The coastal region, the sea islands and the magick drew me in. I was 18 years old when I saw the night lights of Charleston, South Carolina upon the Copper River bridge for the first time and I knew I was home. And now after 40 years of living in and around the region I know where my ashes will be scattered. This is my dirt. My child and grandchild have been born upon this dirt.

Around 14 years old is when my love of the pointy black hat became apparent and gave me quite a sharp turn on my life road. By the time I turned 17 I had found a small group of folk magick / Southern conjure type Witches and practitioners in a nearby town. From there I moved to Charleston, SC, and my studies in magick and folk lore expanded. Also, my love of graveyards really started to develop during this time. I had access to so much history under my feet.

In time I moved to Florence, SC, met Papa Nico, a Haitian Vodou Priest, worked in his shop and he became my mentor. For over 20 years I worked with him daily in his shop and learned about different types of magick from the clients who rely upon the necessities at his botanica. At the same time, I had a coven of Witches coming out to my farm on full moons. Without seeking it, I stood in the crossroads of Traditional Witchcraft, Southern Conjure, Hoodoo and Vodou.

What I realized in this magickal/spiritual journey of mine was that there is a common denominator, dirt. So easy to overlook and yet necessary for every step we take. Through dirt we travel far; sometimes by walking upon it (physical) and sometimes by the journey of the dirt we stand upon (spiritual). Through honor, reverence, and respect, I have walked upon many different dirts and been blessed beyond measure with these connections.

Now, dear reader, look down at the dirt you stand upon and begin your own journey. Remember my words, be inspired, and create a path that is as unique as you.

May your travels take you where you need to be.

Taren S

Chapter 1

Dead, Divine, Sacred

Dead Things

I like dead things. Not freshly or mostly dead, but the truly dead. The remnants of life's essences that lingers within the physical realm and at times seeks to reconnect with the familiar of life we could have or might have known in the physical world. The body we walked with, the hands we held, the cheeks we stroked; skin and flesh depart bone and with time bone turns to silt. What remains after the bones have turned to dust and become apparent only through an energetic connection.

The whispers of forgotten voices in the wind that you can almost hear, a sudden chill when entering a space that tingles energetically in an unfamiliar yet almost familiar way, a lingering scent of signature perfume that wafts by, reminding you of a family member – these are the connections to the Dead that are around us every day. We just need to allow our sixth sense to reveal they have not left us.

As a nine-year-old girl, I not only heard the dead and other worldly spirits, but I talked to them. I remember days walking through the graveyard and laying flowers upon the graves and the conversations that I had with each of the occupants. While I don't remember exactly the content, I had deep dialogues with spiritual residents, seeking to know if they wanted the wildflower bundle I had just picked, or if they deserved it.

As an adult looking back, the line between reality and child fantasy seems too blurred. Today, I am biased with rationales. I imagined the dead or I channeled the dead or the dead appeared before me. There's no way to know for sure. All I can say is that as a child, I was unafraid to walk through the graveyard in Virginia on the way from school to home. If the dead were available to commune, I would've been there communin'. Some people have grandparents, mothers, friends waiting for them after school, and while I had those things, I also had the graveyard to myself. Those surreal moments make me believe that it was all true.

No matter what happened back then, I'm alive now. The present moment is all we have. One day, I will be gone to the grave, ashes scattered to the four corners, returning to the great cycle of life, death, and more life. The process of dirt magick remembers the life sustaining elements within as it obscures the line between decomposition and new growth. When we participate in dirt magick, we do so with reverence for the natural force and mystery that it is.

Dirt reminds us that our physical makeup is made of matter, but we also know that within us lays a measurable amount of energy. Energy is indestructible and does not dissipate. Though a piece of ice can be melted, it cannot be destroyed. Only the form has changed. It becomes water, which can change to smaller particles (steam) or bonded to create ice. Our bodies will be forgotten by all in a physical sense of the former, but we look to the flowers, the weeds, the trees, the moles, the earthworms, the bricks made from mud, the dust storms out West and pollen-covered cars knowing that life does, indeed, go on.

The lesson is no one can make something into nothing. Energy is eternal. The secret of life cannot be explained in material terms. Life can reproduce, but cannot be created. As energy is indestructible, it is logical to assume that the essence of life is indestructible. There are no reasons why life should merely cease because its material instrument has ceased to function. Death happens when life has withdrawn. It now functions on another plane of existence.

The distinguished scientist Sir Oliver Lodge once declared his hypothesis, "... that they (the dead) are all around us in what we call the ether of space rather than in matter; that intercommunication is still possible..." It is well to remember that we are immortal spirits in temporary association with the material.

To one who believes, no explanation is necessary
To one who doubts, no explanation is possible

Before I knew of Sir Oliver, my granny told me that I could commune with the spiritual realm because I held the gift of the Veil. I was somehow connected to liminal spaces and the voices of the dead is what she revealed to me. Full disclosure, she warned me not to seek these otherworldly connects, but remember, I was bold and without the censures of society norms.

I spent many summers with my granny outside of Little Rock, Arkansas, on a rural generational farm. The week I visited occurred during her church's children's summer program or vacation Bible school. We spent the week gluing painted macaroni shells on printed copies of Jesus's face, and when home, I helped granny in her garden, listening to her tell stories.

My affinity with dead and dark entities and energies expanded, working with her in the dirt, hearing her warnings about the crossroads and the rules when traveling through particular crossroads. She told me to respect the dark man in the crossroads and sometimes to fear him. I remember her whispering this to me several times. Granny helped develop my affinity with dead and dark entities and energies unknowingly.

I was thirteen years old when my granny and I were walking down the dirt road back to her house after visiting a friend of hers. On the way, we took the scenic way. "Enjoy the perfect summer afternoon breeze," she told me. The walk was pleasant, and I listened to her fret about the forth coming church cookbook that did not include all the recipes she had summitted. Granny took her recipes and prayers profoundly seriously.

The visit was short, and we started back when granny realized we were running a little behind. She turned and looked quite sternly at me. "We are gonna take a short cut back to the house, but we have to cross through one of the Devil's crossroads. Nothing to be afraid of if you don't look back when walking through" she told me. "We will say the first seven verses of Psalm 91 aloud when we get to the center", was her further instruction.

1 He that dwelleth in the secret place of the most High shall abide under the shadow of the Almighty.
2 I will say of the Lord, He is my refuge and my fortress: my God; in him will I trust.
3 Surely he shall deliver thee from the snare of the fowler, and from the noisome pestilence.
4 He shall cover thee with his feathers, and under his wings shalt thou trust: his truth shall be thy shield and buckler.
5 Thou shalt not be afraid for the terror by night; nor for the arrow that flieth by day;
6 Nor for the pestilence that walketh in darkness; nor for the destruction that wasteth at noonday.
7 A thousand shall fall at thy side, and ten thousand at thy right hand; but it shall not come nigh thee.

I have no idea how many of the Psalms granny had memorized. In my childhood memories I believed she had every verse of biblical scripture in her head. She always had a book, verse, story to cite when making any point worth making. Psalm 91 was one of her go-tos when we needed to bring the light of Divinity closer. Even now when I speak this Psalm aloud, I can hear her voice intoning the words and saying it with me in spirit realm.

Granny was part of the southern primitive Baptist denomination. She would tell me they were the "original

Baptist" with strong beliefs in healings, prayer circles and the power in the word of God (the Bible). They were also a racially intergraded church from the early 1800's which she was quite proud of. She was always part of or planning something at the small country church she attended. Her stories of faith healings and dead folks not really at rest unless you helped them added to my natural affinity towards the netherworlds.

I continued my journeys connecting with spiritual realms as I grew into adulthood. Through research and experience, I learned that there are places that seem to attract spiritual energies and various astral realms. I also came to understand that in some places it accumulates – the strongest places are graveyards, crossroads, and footprints. They all start at the dirt: old graves pushing up trees, footprints left in dirt, and old trodden pathways that we've since paved.

Dirt comes with many categories and sub-categories but for this book I am going to talk about three main categories: Graveyard, Crossroads, and Purposeful (Footprint). Various types of dirt have immensely powerful energy and very practical energies for aiding in magickal works. There are some patterns in folk magick communities regarding using dirts in spiritual and magickal applications. Strangers across continents, belief systems, and backgrounds have come up with similar practices.

We can look to history to see how people have interacted and shared with one another, whether by force or generosity. When you are part of the magickal community at-large, you begin to notice that people are doing what appears to be similar or like-minded workings. Trial and error are one way of figuring it out, channeling is another, and the exchange with the community helps. We're all human, and spirit is spirit. While we are all tied to the life source our understanding of that source will continuously vairy.

There are no lists, however, for the personal connections we create from our own experiences. For example, the dirt of native land, unique "dirts" from places you visit, or natural events like the dust from a volcano. Pop-Up Video reports during an episode featuring *Who Will Save Your Soul* that the singer, Jewel, carries containers of her native Alaskan dirt with her wherever she goes on tour or travels.

It's about personal connection, and the type of personal connection that only you have or can create. If you love someone, dirt from their land might be helpful, but think about what it means to you. Did you love that place? Did you have a terrible break-up with that person? The energy associated with the dirt will translate into the story of the working that you do.

Perhaps the energy of home might be the strongest connection to a place with dirt. We bring a tremendous number of valuable emotions to home and being home creates many emotions within us. It is said that home is where the heart is, and that a house is not a home. What happens in the home reverberates to the rest of our lives. It's that important, and the energy we create at home affects us and the world around us through our experience. Often when people need to fix their lives, they start at home.

In magick, we take it further...we take it into another realm. We use the dirt of home, to change our lives. The reassurance and safety you feel when standing in your family's kitchen. Even years later after your elders are gone, and the house is quiet when you stand in that spot it all returns. Home dirt represents our story: the story of coming into being, of loving, of learning and growing, of creating a family, of sharing the hearth with our closest friends, of creating pillars of strength and respite in times of trouble.

Magick starts at home in the dirt. My kitchen story is Papa Nico's botanica. He has been my friend and mentor for almost 30 years now. His botanica is my going home story. When I return and the door opens, I feel like I can breathe deeply and for real. We all need that special place that brings us a sense of wholeness; completely grounded in who you are in that moment.

The magickal feeling you get after a long day, when you come in, greet your pets, family, roommate, partner, or your perfect silence and peace, is the magick we use with home. It's protecting, comforting, solid. One can rely on the dirt at home, where you can truly be yourself. This magick uses authenticity. Do you want to create a new story, a new job, a new life? Get to know yourself, know deep down what you truly want, and make magick with the dirt beneath your feet.

Divine Dirt

There is something special and sacred about the land we come from. It's the land our ancestors lived on, the land that has shaped our cultures and identities. And it's the land we call home. When we embrace our regional, cultural, and ancestral ties to the land, we are tapping into a powerful source of strength, connection and belonging. We are more than our cities, our states and even our countries. Our roots stretch deep back into the land, connecting us to a rich heritage that we can be proud of.

By exploring our regional, cultural, and ancestral ties to the land, we strive to understand and appreciate the ways in which it has shaped us. We also build connections with others who share these ties – communities of people across geographical boundaries that come together around a common bond. And as we celebrate the land that we stand on today, we can find pride in our heritage and the stories it holds. We don't have to look to other people traditions to find our own because our traditions are right in our backyard and right under our feet.

The land that we are standing on is more than just a place. It's more than just where our feet rest against the earth or how much grass reaches upwards to our knees. It's a place that harbors our heritage, our culture, and the history of those who came before us. This is a place that is highly unique to each individual person. For some, it might be the vast open plains of their homeland in Canada or Australia. For others, it might be the crowded streets of an inner city. And for others, it might be a rural farm down a dirt road off a dirt road.

No matter where you are from or what your connection is to the land, it's important to remember that we all come from somewhere. We all have a connection to the land, whether we realize it or not. Think about your own connection to the land. What does it mean to you? What are your earliest memories of the land you grew up on? What is your favorite place on the land you currently live? Take some time to really think about your connection to the land and what it means to you. It's a special bond that we all share and it's important to honor it and embrace it.

Looking back on my childhood, I have always had a deep connection to the land that I grew up on. Whether it was walking through the forests near my house, playing in the grassy fields at the edge of town, or strolling along the seashore, there has always been a sense of peace and calm that I felt when I was connected to the land. Whenever I am troubled or feeling lost, I seek these connections, no matter where I am in the moment.

As an adult, I still feel that same sense of connection. Even though I now live outside a major city, I still try to get out into nature as often as I can. It's important for me to stay connected to the land and embrace the unique history and culture that I come from. No matter where you are or what your relationship is to the land, it's important to remember and honor this connection. Embrace your heritage, culture, and ancestral ties to the land we all stand on. As Gandhi once said, "earth provides enough to satisfy every man's need but not for every man's greed". So, let's make an effort to respect this amazing gift from nature and remember to cherish it always.

When it comes to connecting with the land you stand on, it's important to remember that there is both good and bad to this relationship. Just as the land can provide us with a sense of peace and calm, it can also be the source of conflict and pain.

For example, while many people might feel a strong connection to their home country, others might have complicated feelings about the land they come from. This is often the case for people who have experienced war or violence in their homeland. In these cases, it's important to remember that there can be a range of different feelings associated with the land we stand on.

It's also important to remember that our connection to the land is not static – it can change over time. For example, a person might feel a strong connection to their home country when they are living there, but that connection might change if they move to another country. Similarly, our connection to the land might also change as we experience different life events or meet new people.

Overall, it's important to remember that our connection to the land is complex and ever-changing. While the land can provide us with a sense of peace and calm, it can also be the source of conflict and pain. It's important to be aware of both the good and bad when it comes to our relationship with the land we stand on. And remember we can't run from or ignore the bad – but must instead face it and try to create a better future for ourselves and those around us. Once we know better it is our job to do better.

So, whether you're embracing the good or dealing with the bad when it comes to connecting with the land you stand on, remember that this dynamic relationship is an important part of our lives. And by embracing the good and dealing with the bad, we can come to better understand our connection to this amazing natural resource. After all, we are all connected to the land – for better or for worse.

Sacred Dirt

Within a handful of dirt we find the entirety of the universe; there is both life and death, instantaneously and simultaneously happening as you are holding it. There are things growing and there are things rotting. The possibility of things to come, and the ending of others. Take a moment to channel possibilities that might be in a handful of dirt.

What comes up in your mind? An entity might be giving you the information, and maybe it is the person, animal spirit, or other worldly entities that now resides, in part, in the dirt. Maybe you receive a message or feeling of comfort or maybe holding the dirt gets you in a space of magickal reverence or spiritual connection to realms unseen. How you use it is up to you.

Perhaps you have only thought about dirt when you are trying to vacuum it out of the floor mats of the car or the carpets in your house (or, if you're lucky, watching someone else do it) never realizing dirt is full of magickal energies. It has the power to support a wide variety of your magickal intentions, and it can store all kinds of energy depending on where you get your dirt from and how you would like to use it. Look at what it has already done, made a way, blown in, hitched a ride into your home. It's practically begging to be noticed, entertained, honored. Study what's in the dustpan, cut open your vacuum cleaner bag outside to see what's accumulated. Ask a question before digging in and tossing it in the air. Do you get an answer? Think about what is in a handful of 'good' dirt and all that it represents.

For some folks who hear the everyday whisper of magick there is an understanding of the true power of dirt and how to use it. The type of dirt will dictate how it will be used for magickal purposes or spiritual connections and it will tell you if you are attuned and listening. Dirt that has lots of life in it containing roots, seeds, organic material will be used differently than dirt that has little life in it, opened from bags, put in sandboxes, sterilized, and dyed for an aquarium. With the latter, there might be an opportunity to imbue it for a life-sustaining purpose should you be so inclined. Mixing it with a plant for a season, taking it out of an aquarium that once hosted a robust collection of fish, ornamental dirt that has been worked this way makes for wonderful life changing dynamics.

Sacred Dirt could be classified as a working man's magickal ingredient. Working man's magick is everyday magick that you can use on the go without the fuss of ritual. Try a small pinch of dirt under a ritual candle, add an extra "something-something" to a mojo bag, or sprinkle for protection in corners. It can be used to make your magick more grounded, centered, and powerful.

Chapter 2

Purposeful Dirt

Purposeful Dirt is probably the most common and easily accessible of all the magickal dirts. It is also extremely versatile, making it great for various workings and/or spell work whether they be light or dark. It really comes down to an individual's connection to dirt and creativity.

There are all sorts of ways to use purposeful dirt. It can be used for protection, cleansing, healing and of course, cursing and hexing. In some cases, it can be used as an offering or a sacrifice. It really does just depend on what the practitioner is trying to achieve.

Dirt also has a long history and association to fertility and growth. This makes it ideal for use in workings related to these matters. It can also be used to help manifest other desires such as wealth, success, prosperity, or love. Such as, the dirt from a plant that is known to promote fertility can used in a working to help someone conceive. Or the dirt from a bank could be used in workings to attract wealth and abundance.

When working with purposeful dirt, be creative and intuitively aligned (follow your gut). There are no hard and fast rules other than mindfulness and reverence of the dirt. The key to using purposeful dirt is to be creative, respectful, and open to possibilities. There are endless ways to let our imaginations run wild.

Magickal Uses for Dirt

Dirt from your home is a simple and effortless way to get started with using dirt in your magickal workings. This dirt represents "Spirit of place" and will stand in for your home and the people who live there in any working you do. Use this dirt in all your protection workings/spells. Gather from the front doorsteps or entrance most commonly used.

Cleansing

It might sound counterintuitive, but you can use dirt to cleanse your magickal tools before or after any magickal work. To do this, dig a hole in your garden or backyard and bury whatever magickal tools you need to cleanse in the dirt. Leave them in the ground for at least one night. Then dig them up, rinse them off, and use them for your next working.

If you need to put your magickal tools through a deep cleanse, leave your tools buried in the dirt for a full lunar cycle. If you do not have access to a yard or garden spot, you can bury your magickal tools in a pot of dirt for cleansing. Place the pot outside or by a window so it can absorb the lunar energy overnight.

Banishing

Burying items in dirt can also be an excellent way to do a banishing working. To do this, write a word or draw a sigil that represents what you need to banish on a rock, a piece of paper, or a bay leaf. You can banish anything you want. You could banish an emotion you no longer want to feel, a person in your life who is bothering you, or a fear that is holding you back.

Once you have written on your rock or paper, hold the object between your palms and visualize the energy of whatever you're trying to banish moving from your body, out of your hands and into the object. Bury the object in the dirt and leave it in there. If you ever wish to reverse your working, you can dig up the object you buried. This magickal working is recommended to do during the dark or waning moon.

Dirt is also known for banishing a hex called the Evil Eye. If you suspect someone has cursed you, you can collect dirt from the four corners of your home and mix it all together. Then you stand outside the front door of your home and throw the dirt as far away from your home as possible, shouting for the Evil Eye to get out of your space.

Other Dirts and Their Uses

Bank

The sayings "dirty rich" and "dirt cheap" come to mind. When you are doing money or prosperity workings, make sure that you're in the right place in your mind especially if you add dirt to the working. Sometimes the opposite of what you want can be best, like getting something "dirt cheap." Be open to change when using dirt. Sometimes the best things grow slowly while devil's foot weed can spring up overnight. Take dirt from around the bank's shrubbery, be sure not to take the decorative red mulch, and put the dirt at the bottom of your money tin, jar, or wherever you keep your change to help it grow.

Your Garden

You already know the myriad of benefits that your garden provides you and your land. The flowers attract bees that pollenate the world. The growth attracts wildlife. You grow things that can be used to treat burns, colds, heart disease. Moving around the garden offers a chance for exercise. Being under the sun gives your body a chance to produce vitamin D. The dirt holds all that energy.

Sprinkle dirt from your garden while walking around the outside of your house seven times repeating Psalm 89:11.

The heavens are thine, the earth also is thine: as for the world and the fulness thereof, thou hast founded them.

Enemies Garden

In New Orleans there is a beautiful neighborhood called the Garden District. It is full of grand houses from one era mixed with turn of the century cottages from another era, all surrounded in lush greenery and plantings. A couple of years ago I took one of the walking tours through this area and the tour guide told us the following story:

The Garden District was created as a millionaire's playground of vacation or second/third homes with no expenses spared. McMansions of various types with ornate water fountains, statues imported from far off places and swanky gardens designed by world renown fancy folk people flanked the streets from each other creating the beginning of the Garden District.

One of the early residents was a railroad magnate from up north trying to relocate to New Orleans with too much money to spend and wanting to show it off. James Robb created a show place villa in 1851 taking up an entire block of Washington Ave. Folks referred to him as the Father of the Garden district because of his palace of a home and lavish landscapings. His gardens were breathtaking from afar and for a few of the privileged a stroll through the living art was possible.

Also, he was an ass and was a member of the pro-slavery council in New Orleans. Needless to say, most local folks did not hold a high opinion of him. It is also said his gardener was the same, both proud with quite a reputation of superiority. The story is that he/they refused to share one clipping of the many plants throughout his gardens with any of his neighbors. He seemed to like folks being jealous of what he had, and they didn't.

By the late 1870's, his wife had died and in the early 1880's, he lost most of his fortune and moved back north leaving the house empty. During this time local and neighbor folks took clippings from his gardens and planted them in their own yards creating the Garden District you see today.

The moral/magick of this story is in the dirt. Taking dirt from the garden of an enemy and creating something of beauty is the ultimate revenge. Let your success be their downfall.

Wanting to Move

On the internet, you can buy dirt from anywhere you wish to move, but I encourage you to visit a place, physically, to get a feel for it. If it feels right, scoop up a bit of dirt from a graveyard, crossroads, your own footprints or from a place that feels right and work it to bring yourself to a point of moving onward and outward. Draw a map of where it is you want to live, the state, the county, the neighborhood. Put the dirt from that place on top of it. Place near a white candle that you light every full moon or when you feel like it.

Your Place of Employment

Tired of getting passed over for that promotion? Need a raise? Dirt from your place of employment can massively add to workings of this nature. It's also useful to hex that co-worker or boss who just won't give you a break. Add a dab of dirt to your desk or table under a cotton cloth and place your laptop, notebook, rolodex, calendar on it to ground your work, make contacts, or achieve perfect timing.

Hospital

Hospitals try to create spaces of solace, spirituality, silence to balance the phrenetic energy in them. Look for the oases of courtyards with waterfalls, the chapels, the bereavement rooms. Take dirt from potted plants if the plant in them is living. Use dust from the pews. Add hospital dirt to amulets for good health. It can be used for both healing and harm.

Courthouse

Courts create spaces for honor and respect amidst personal turmoil. People swear on the bible, pray, cry, shout, lose freedom, get equality, get what's fair, get what's coming to them. Collect county court dirt for workings of justice or legal matters. Sprinkle it on top of a "get out of jail" candle. Lay a mirror down and sprinkle dirt on it to increase charisma. Put your bible in the center of a room and lay it on top of a white cotton cloth under which is court dirt and ask for justice.

Sole of your Foot

If you think about bringing your foot down on someone's neck or even their hand, pinning them to the ground, you could temporarily have control over them. Scrape up some dirt from the sole of your shoe to use in command, and control workings. Write their name on a piece of paper, fold the paper three times and then three more times the other way. Wrap it with a black string and sprinkle with dirt to bring them under your command.

Dirt from the River's Edge

In many Afro-Caribbean traditions river water is the natural manifestation of the Loa (Goddess) of Love and lasting relationships, Oshun. Offerings are left for her by the water's edge. Louisiana Vodou teaches that when working love, your working deals with you first.

The Mountains

"May your dreams be larger than mountains and may you have the courage to scale their summits." – Harley King

Use dirt from mountains in workings of ambition, overcoming obstacles and creating longevity. Also use in communicating with the spirits that reside specifically in a mountain region. The nature of mountains involves seeing around hills and valleys. In *Enlightened*, Amy thinks of her friends, family, coworkers who seem to have more than she does. Spiritually, she stands in a valley. Depending on where you stand, in the Great Smokies or Sandia, the sun can shine while casting long shadows across the land. Compel yourself to experience what you know is there yet cannot see. Amy knows that just because she sees darkness, that a brighter truth exists. Put some dirt in your hand, and say, "I will not wait for the sun. It is all around me" to cast out dark energies.

The Forest

The forest contains mysteries. The flora and fauna become varied based on where the sun hits or does not hit. Soft moss protected from the sun can flourish. It can take over rock, plants, until it exposes itself to sun and dries up. Used in workings of protection.

Home of a Witch

Let's hope that you are friends with a Witch and can ask permission to take some of their dirt. Great, now you can fill a doll in the likeness of someone you do not care for with the dirt and poke it with needles, keep it on the toilet to induce nausea, or give it to your dogs. Witch dirt is for workings of domination & harm. And no, you can't have dirt from my yard; just stating this for the record.

12 Noon

Gather your dirt at noon but save it for workings at midnight. Dirt in the daytime has a different quality because the sun bakes it. The flora and fauna changes subtly throughout the day. When the sun is blaring down, sensitive animals and flowers fold into the ground and into themselves, waiting for cooler weather and less sun. Try putting small bags of noon dirt in your shoes when walking into a tense situation at work, court, or even down the aisle on your wedding day. This will help you be in the right place at the right time.

Seashore

For fertility and cleansing workings. Try filling a decorative fishbowl with dirt from the seashore and filling it with fresh water. Change it regularly to keep it clear. Water will increase your sexuality.

Where Two Dogs Have Fought

If you have dogs, you know they sometimes fight. If you have friends with dogs, ask them about it. A friend of mine has one dog, but on a walk, a neighbor's dog got loose and attacked his dog while on a walk. Everything worked out, but he knows where it happened. Use dirt from that area for workings of conflict.

Sprinkle some on a picture of a couple you want to break up, throw some over the fence in your neighbor's yard (though the conflict might be with you), fill a black no-show sock with dirt and sew it shut. Drive by and throw it in a yard, send it in the mail, leave it on a desk of your target to put them in a state of conflict.

Casino

If you take a trip to Vegas or Atlantic city, don't take the dirt for granted. Gather some for your workings or ask a friend you trust who is going to get some for you. For fast money workings, like lighting a money candle and putting it out in a saucer of casino dirt. These workings don't come without risk as in gambling.

Law library

States have law schools, and law schools have legal libraries. A lawyer or judge friend might have a library in his or her home. You can use dirt from your law friend's home if you have to. What we need is dirt carrying the heady energy of the knowledge of the law, good law, fair law. Ambulance chasing or turning over laws for the sake of turning over the law is not the dirt you want to use.

In the US, the justice system is designed for equality and fairness. It falls short as all human institutions do, but it is hard to name a better system. Help the system where you live along with law library dirt legal matters. Your legal matter is probably taking over your life or, at least, your free time. Add it to your altar. Add a copy of the Constitution to your altar while you're at it. Add a photo of Benjamin Franklin. Channel his wisdom and his mystical qualities as he published the *Poor Richard's Almanac*.

Library

As one of the last free places to exist, this dirt will be easy to collect. Make sure it's a library that still has physical copies of books because some are fully digital. Use library dirt for knowledge & wisdom. Add it to your altar. Put it in a beautiful dish or an old dish or a handmade dish or all the beforementioned, setting the dish on top of your bookshelf.

Doctors' Office

Take some dirt from a potted plant or from near the plantings outside. If it's an old, standalone building, use the dirt from anywhere on the property. Do you see the doctor's parking space? Collect sand from there or dirt from around the car. Put it in a doll with the likeness of yourself for workings of healing.

Once on *Oprah*, a woman used a statue of Beatrix Kiddo from *Kill Bill* to manifest healing from cancer. Set her on top of a bit of dirt on your nightstand, so she can have a steady footing as she swings her Hattori Hanzo sword in your sleep.

4 points weave the spell,
East, South, West, and North,
Is your tale to tell

Dirt from 4 Banks

Use your favorite Queen of Swords from tarot to trace a likeness on paper. Color the whole thing in celebratory colors, using lots of green and purple. Find a small coin purse to put in your picture and dirt from the four banks. Make sure to keep this one your altar until you feel it is time to remove it. You will know when prosperity comes in a given situation.

4 Churches

The dirt from four different churches mixed together is an immensely powerful ingredient to be used in cleansing workings. If you make your own cologne or perfume, add dirt to the mixture, but you might also add a little to your favorite fragrance. Get a sample sprayer from Macy's or Belk to use around the house, when facing a dire situation with a bad person or if a good person is in a bad mood and the area needs an uplift after their visit.

4 Corners of a Crossroad

To open the roads of success, keep in a beautiful container of this dirt near your front door. This correlates with Ellegua, keeper of the crossroads. If you cannot make your container, get one you love that is handcrafted. If you cannot find a handcrafted one you love, choose an oblong container that you can make your own through painting, decorating, or repurposing in some way. Fill it with dirt. Get a second container and repeat near your bedroom door, your backdoor, your safe.

Dirt from 4 jails

Used in workings to either release or keep an individual incarcerated. I once did a "Stay in jail, you're a shit" working using this mixture. Later it was revealed that the person stayed in jail for quite a while due to paperwork problems. I ain't say anything, but just saying.

4 Police Stations

Dirt from police stations might be collect from many precincts in many towns across the country. If an old police station becomes a memorial, don't overlook this dirt. It might represent those who have already lived and would like just one more shot to take down an evildoer or someone who crossed you that really doesn't want their business investigated. On the other hand, police presence can be a moderating force in a dangerous location. Like all crossroads, it can go either way.

Manifesting with Dirt

Dirt has the natural ability to nurture and grow. This energy is useful in manifesting workings. If you have a big project or goal you would like to accomplish in the coming months, write out that goal on a slip of paper. Write it in first person and present tense, starting with "I", and focusing on the positive outcomes of the goal. For example: "I am an extremely successful business owner." Bury that slip of paper in a pot or in your garden along with a seed. As your plant grows, your goal will manifest. I like to do this with annual herbs (Thyme, Chives, Basil are my favs) because they grow quickly, and they are easy to take care of.

Footprint Dirt

This dirt is used when you are doing a working on a specific person, namely whoever's footprint you have. I have seen this dirt used as an ingredient in love spells, protection charms, and magickal workings of commanding and compelling. Gather up the footprint dirt and place in a paper bag. Foot track magick is mentioned in Greek, Hebrew, and African sources. There are two main ways to use footprints:

- To do something to the footprint found in the ground, to hex or curse the person who left it.

- Gather dirt from the footprint to use in a magickal working.

One can use someone's footprint to banish them from returning or to instead encourage them to return. Perhaps a lover has left a little too hastily, might you want to lace their footprint with aphrodisiacs so they might return to you soon?

In the novel *Call Me By Your Name* by Andre Aciman, Elio steps in Oliver's footsteps in the sand. He said that he was pining for him. Being so in love, Elio connected to his deep self and expanded his being using what he felt. He did what felt right at the time. Stepping into Oliver's footsteps placed him in the presence of his love even though his love wasn't there, only steps away. This foretold the ending of their relationship and how might Elio achieve divine connection to Oliver once he returned to America.

Think about how you might use a footprint. If you do not have a person's footprint, trace your own and write your name on one and the other name on your other foot. Cut them out and place this pointed towards your door, not away from it.

A participant in a *House of Witchcraft* Zoom call told me about a tradition in India where the new wife walks through sand or red powder into the husband's home. Depending on where she went, determines if the mother-in-law would like her or not. Try using talcum powder or clove oil on the bottom of your feet and walking through your house to represent where you want your love to go. You could put on their socks and/or shoes and walk around the house...or out of the house.

Remember, it is of utmost importance with any footprint working to get the right footprint. You do not want do sex magick on the mail carrier or your father-in-law, and you don't want to banish your daughter when you meant to keep the Avon sales lady away.

Dirt Spells And Workings

To Release Someone from Jail
Place a picture of the imprisoned person on a white plate. Sprinkle over it Deerhorn powder & powdered Palo Abre Camino. Place a large skeleton key on picture. Sprinkle dirt from the forest and then dirt from four jails over the photo. Burn a red 7-day candle or Saint Expedite candle that has been anointed with "Get out of Jail" oil by the plate. Put a small drop of this oil in candle daily. On the 8th day, wrap all the items in a white cloth and dispose of near the jailed individual.

Get out of Jail Oil
2 oz. Castor oil, 3 drops of vervain and nutmeg oil, 7 drops of calamus oil.

Another Working to Release Someone from Jail
Place imprisoned person's picture or tag locks (hair, nail clippings, footprint dirt) on a plate. Sprinkle dirt from four jails over the photo. Burn a red 7-day candle beside the plate. Recite the verses daily and say the person's name aloud three times.

> Psalm 142 verses 6 & 7
> *Attend unto my cry; for I am brought very low: deliver me from my persecutors; for they are stronger than I.*
> *bring my soul out of prison, that I may praise thy name: the righteous shall encompass me; for thou shalt deal bountifully with me*

To Keep Someone in Jail
Place photo of individual on a white plate and sprinkle with herbs of the dead (your choice, see herb section). Sprinkle dirt from four cemeteries then the dirt from four police stations over the photo. Burn a black 7-day candle that has been anointed

with a commanding or domination oil. On the 8th day, bury the items near a jail.

To Dominate an Individual

Place photo of individual on a white plate and sprinkle with dirt form the bottom of your shoe. Sprinkle dirt from four cemeteries over the photo. Burn a black 7-day candle that has been anointed with a commanding or domination oil by the plate. Put a small drop of the oil in candle daily. On the 8th day, wrap the items in a red cloth and bury in a wooded area.

To Cause Conflicts

Write the individuals name six times on a piece of brown paper bag and insert nine needles into the paper and then place on a white plate. Sprinkle a mixture of black cat & black dog fur over the paper. Next, sprinkle separation or confusion powder and then dirt from where two dogs have fought over the paper. Burn a black 7-day candle that has been anointed with separation or confusion oil by the plate. Put a small drop of the oil in candle daily. On the 8th day, wrap the items and dispose of in the back corner of a graveyard.

To Escape the Law

Write the person's name seven times on a piece of brown paper bag, place on a plate and sprinkle it with cascarilla (powdered eggshell) and Deerhorn powder. Next, sprinkle the paper with dirt from four churches & dirt from a forgotten graveyard. Light a "Law Stay Away" 7-day candle that has been anointed with "Law Stay Away" Oil by the plate. Place a drop of this oil in candle daily. On the 8th day, bury the contents in your yard.

To Bring the Police

Place dirt from four police stations, dirt from four street corners, dirt from a courthouse and dirt from four cemeteries in a mixing bowl and mix. Light a black 7-day candle that has been anointed with a jinx or crossing-type oil by the bowl. Put a drop of this oil in candle daily. On the eighth day, sprinkle all of the dirt from the bowl at the individual's home or business that you want the police to go to.

To Protect Your Home from Enemies

Mix dirt from the forest, dirt from four churches, dirt from a forgotten graveyard, dirt from a soldier's grave, dirt from a Holy person's home and one tablespoon Deerhorn powder together in a large mixing bowl. Light a 7 African Powers (rainbow) 7-day candle anointed with protection-type oil by the mixing bowl. Put a small drop of the oil in the candle daily. On the 8th day, sprinkle the contents of the bowl around your home and property. Follow up with a complete cleaning and mopping of the house with a Protection-type floor wash and carpet sweep.

Protection Floor Wash

1 cup Hyssop,
1 cup Basil,
1 cup Peppermint,
1 cup Lemongrass,
1 cup Sage (fresh, if possible, dried will do)

Boil all the ingredients in one quart of water for 20 minutes. After liquid has cooled, strain off the liquid. Then add to it, 1 cup of ammonia, 1/2 cup Florida water & 1/2 cup salt. Place in a plastic bottle and leave for seven days before using. Wash all your floors with the mixture.

For the carpet sweep, simply powder all the herbs and mix with the salt & some baking soda. Mixture is sprinkled over the carpet and can then be either swept across rug and out the door or vacuumed up while concentrating on your desire.

To Make an Individual Move

Mix dirt from 4 cemeteries and dirt where two dogs have fought together in a mixing bowl. Add some "Hot Foot" or "Get Away" powder to the mixture. Light a black 7-day candle instilled with "Hot Foot" or "Get Away" oil by the mixing bowl & recite the Prayer of the Intranquil Spirit. Instill a bit of the oil in the candle daily and recite the prayer. On the 8th day, sprinkle the contents of the bowl on the persons property or where they are sure to walk over it.

"O' Intranquil Spirit, you that in hell are wandering and will never reach heaven hear me, O' hear me!

I want you to grasp the five senses of (name of target) and do not let him rest in peace, neither seated nor standing, waking nor sleeping, that he should find himself as desperate as the waters of the seas and as torn as the wind in the storm until he moves.

(Name of target), I conjure you before the cross and God Almighty that you are move away as quickly as the living after the cross and the dead after the light.

Amen."

Spirit of Place

Spirit is the essence of a place, object, or creature. It is the life-force, the animating principle that gives rise to all things. In humans, it's the soul. In plants, it's the root. For places and other worldly beings, it is the spirit of place.

There is something special about certain places – a feeling, an atmosphere, a sense of peace or calm and sometimes fear. We may not be able to put our finger on it, but we know it when we feel it. This is the spirit of place. Some believe that the land itself has a spirit. Places can have good spirits and/or bad spirits. A place with a good spirit is often called sacred, while a place with a bad spirit is said to be cursed.

Some folks believe that the spirit of place is affected by the events that have taken place there. If something has happened, the spirit of place may be "tainted" by it. For example, if there has been a murder, suicide or battle at a location, many folks believe that the spirit of place will be forever changed. Others believe that the spirit of place is something that has always been there, regardless of what has happened. This may be because they believe that the land itself has a spirit, or because they feel a connection to the history of a place. As one saying goes. "If these walls could talk: we would hear stories." Places have spirit and they echo through time.

It is the spirit of a place, the essential personality, bringing a place to life. Quite frequently we experience this unknowingly. Think of place that instantly brings peace, happiness, pain, or sadness. For example, a church or prisoners of war camps. These places carry significant levels of energy that has in essence created a whole spirit.

The spirit becomes ingrained and invested in these places. I lived in a historic house in Murfreesboro, North Carolina for a very short time because the lady of the house did not care for me. Rumor has it Ms. Lassiter was found dead in the house under mysterious circumstances in the 1850's. Prior to her death, an enslaved black servant around the 1810's had hung herself in one of the closets in a small bedroom upstairs.

I was in residence at the home as a historical revitalization project in the late 1980's thinking that I was creating my forever home. Ms. Lassiter, who was very dead, made it very clear that was never going to happen. The story of the house is a 250 plus years dark history of insanity, divorce, and death. Somehow the house constantly stayed in a state of empty with family after family having situations (some quite mysterious) forcing them to leave. I was the longest occupant in that house in 40 years.

Upon moving into this house, I knew someone or something otherworldly lived there. I thought to appease the spirits and left offerings and started keeping a journal on the activity. Doors opening rather forcefully and then slamming shut, kitchen drawers that were closed found ajar or windows now mysteriously opened, and loud sounds of footsteps on the staircases at 3 a.m. most nights became my norm as the spirits in the house made their presence known.

I said prayers, cast protection circles and built altars for Ms. Lassiter and the other spirits hoping to help bring peace. Every altar was destroyed. None of them wanted to make peace or accept that I would for any significant period staying in the house. The back and forth between us finally ended with me shouting one night, "Okay you win, I am moving out." And then all was eerily quiet.

Once I started packing all activity stopped and stayed that way until I was out of the house. I am happy to say that the property has been fully renovated although no one has been able to live there for any significant amount of time. Quite recently, I found out that the house was up for sale again. Any offers?

Her spirit claimed that house very powerfully. She will stay its guardian and keep whatever she deems unfit out. We also hear about these stories in movies and tv shows. *The House on Haunted Hill* and *The Others*, tell the story of the souls that are in fact the home. The first season of *American Horror Story* features a house that trapped the spirits of all who died in it.

Some became guardians of the house. Sarah Paulson's character, a medium, talks about the spirit, in so many words, about how malevolent spirits can rule a place. This also foreshadows the second season where lots of mysterious, evil, and good things happen in an asylum.

In many indigenous cultures, the land is seen as a living being with its own spirit. Therefore, many indigenous people have a strong connection to their land. They believe that the land is a part of them, and they are a part of the land. This connection is at the heart of their culture and their way of life. In folklore magick there are many of the same.

One of my great grand uncles worked in the mines of West Virginia for a brief time and came home to tell the story of the Tommyknockers. According to the family story he heard the knocking and then the alarm sounded for a cave in. All the miners were able to get out of the depths and to safety in time. Shortly after that my great uncle came home to Arkansas and went back to farming. The spirits warned him of the danger while not being a danger themselves.

My granny loved to tell the story of her favorite uncle and his experience with the local spirits of place, the Tommyknockers, found in the mine. She said when he heard the first knock he turned as white as a ghost and a deep chill went down his spine. On the second knock his feet could not move fast enough to get out of the shaft. She said he would tell folks that he heard a voice telling him to "leave now!" and he did.

The story of the Tommyknocker is an old, old folktale with seemingly contemporary origins from the British Isles. There are many variations of this tale. Tommyknockers are good spirits, or they are evil spirits. They are fairy folk with mischievous natures, or they are spirits of dead miners. Knackers or Bucca, in Cornwall, are like Brownies or Leprechauns. Wales calls them Bwca, but no matter their name, Tommyknockers protect miners. It is said that the creatures are no more than two feet tall, and they dress like the miners.

You must keep an eye on them. Great protectors they might be, but they will steal unattended food and tools as well. Yet when a cave-in is imminent, they save the miners by their knocking.

Miners must deal with poisonous gases, carbon monoxide and other hazards. And always miners needed to stay vigilant for the constant threat of collapses. The Tommyknockers are there to help them.

Such warnings give the miners the time to escape from being buried deep within the earth with little to no chance of recovery. They will appear in-person to a beloved miner to show them the way out of the mine. As a thank you, the miners will leave part of their meals out. A common offering, still used to this day, is leaving baked small Saffron cakes as gifts to the Tommyknockers.

The Tommyknockers migrated with the Cornish Miners to Pennsylvania. They then migrated from Pennsylvania to the southern Appalachian mines. From there they made their way to the gold mines of California. Miners believe in Tommyknockers strongly.

They will not work at a mine unless they know the Tommyknocker is there. The descendants of Cornish miners petitioned the owners of a California mine to open the mine to let the Tommyknockers out when it closed in 1956. The miners wanted to free the Tommyknockers from the mine. This is done to ensure, the Tommyknocker could go to another mine to protect other miners. Intriguingly, the owners agreed.

Types of Spirit of Place

There are many different types of spirit of place. Some of the most common include:

- Ancestral Spirits
- Nature Spirits
- Guardian Spirits
- Healing Spirits
- Ancient Wisdom Keepers
- Land Spirits

Ancestral Spirits

Ancestral spirits are the spirits of our ancestors. They can be the spirit of a specific ancestor, or the spirit of our ancestors as a whole. They can be a source of guidance, comfort, and support. They can help us to connect with our culture and our history.

Nature Spirits

Nature spirits are the spirits of the natural world. They can be the spirit of a specific plant, animal, or element. They can also be the spirit of the natural world as a whole. They can be a source of guidance, comfort, and support. They can help us to connect with the natural world and our place within it.

Guardian Spirits

Guardian spirits are protective spirits. They can be the spirit of a specific place or thing. They can also be the spirit of a specific person or group of people. Guardian spirits can help us to feel safe and protected. They can also help us to connect with our sense of purpose.

Healing Spirits

Healing spirits are the spirits of healing. They can be the spirit of a specific place or thing. They can also be the spirit of a specific person or group of people. Healing spirits can help us to heal our wounds, both physical and emotional. They can also help us to connect with our sense of wholeness.

Ancient Wisdom Keepers

Ancient wisdom keepers are the spirits of ancient wisdom. They can be the spirit of a specific place or thing. They can also be the spirit of a specific person or group of people. Ancient wisdom keepers can help us to connect with the wisdom of the ages. They can also help us to connect with our own innate wisdom.

Land Spirits

Land spirits are the spirits of the land. They can be the spirit of a specific place or thing. They can also be the spirit of the land as a whole. Land spirits can help us to connect with the land. They can also help us to connect with our sense of place within the world.

Haints

This might be the most popular magickal lore turned tradition found in the southern region of America. It started within the Gullah community, descendants of former enslaved black folks found in the coastal region of South Carolina and Georgia. These folks believed that haints, angry spirits trapped between the world of the living and the dead would try to enter their houses.

But spirits can't cross water. So instead of building a moat around their house, they created watery pigments, the blue-green color we now know as haint blue, to paint the entry ways of their homes to confuse and trick the spirits into thinking they can't enter.

The term "hant" is an old Gullah word referring to a ghostly presence. Over the years, "hant" turned into "haint" and it stuck. This popular belief has most southern folks painting their porch ceilings "Haint Blue" to ward off evil spirits. What started as a magickal working for protection is now considered a traditional southern color you paint the ceiling of your porch with. There are several paint and hardware stores in the Lowcountry area that offer pre-blended paints named in varying hues of this magickal color. My favorite color is "Miss Celica's Porch."

It is also worth noting that wasps and mosquitos don't like the color either. It has been proved to repel them.

Boo Hags

'Don't let de hag ride ya'

One of the beliefs that Gullahs hold is that people have both a soul and a spirit. They believe that souls leave human bodies upon death, and, if it's a good soul, it ascends to Heaven. The spirit of a person has a different function. A good spirit stays behind to watch over the deceased's family, guiding and protecting them, if needed.

A bad spirit, on the other hand, is a "boo hag." The boo hag uses witchcraft to manipulate people and steal energy from the living while they sleep. Gullahs sometimes bid each other good night, saying "don't let de hag ride ya!"

According to Gullah legend, Boo hags are undead beings that feed off living humans, sort of like vampires. They are skinless, so to survive in the world of the living, they'll steal a living person's skin, and wear it so that they can move about without suspicion. At night, though, they shed the skin, and go looking for a victim to "ride."

Boo hags are crafty creatures. They can get into your house through very small opening, like keyholes. Once inside, they'll sit on a sleeping victim's chest, and steal their breath, or, more specifically, their energy. A boo hag will "ride" its victim all night long, then sneak away before dawn to return to its skin. If it can't get back to its skin before the sun comes up...poof... it will be destroyed. If you've ever woken up exhausted after a full night's rest, you may have been visited by a boo hag.

Like other evil spirits in Gullah culture, boo hags are repelled by shades of indigo blue (haint blue). Painting the ceilings of your porches haint blue will discourage boo hags from stopping at your house. Salt, too, is a good boo hag repellent.

Also, they can't seem to pass a straw broom by without counting every last strand. By the time they finish counting, they typically don't have enough time to get back to their skin before the sun comes up. Sieves and strainers will also work, because they'll need to count all the holes. Some boo hags can count fast, so you might want to keep a few bristled brushes and strainers around.

Working With Spirit of Place

When we connect with the spirit of place, we are connecting with something much larger than ourselves. We are tapping into a deep well of wisdom and knowledge. We are also opening ourselves up to the possibility of healing and transformation. The spirit of place can offer us guidance, comfort, and support. It can help us to feel connected to something larger than ourselves. It can also help us to connect with our ancestors and the land that they come from.

When we connect with the spirit of place, we are creating a deep connection to the land that we will live on. This connection can be a source of strength and inspiration. It can help us to feel connected to our community and to the natural world. It can also help us to feel connected to our history and the history of the land. If feeling lost, disconnected, or just stuck in life, connecting with the spirit of place can offer a sense of grounding and connection. Providing a guided path back to ourselves.

Connecting With Spirit of Place

There are many ways to connect with the spirit of place. One way is to spend time in nature and allow yourself to be open to the experience. Places that have been considered sacred for centuries are often particularly powerful. Take some time to sit or walk in silence and see what comes up for you. Pay attention to your surroundings and see if you can sense anything special about the place.

Another way to connect with the spirit of place is through history. Learn about the land and the people who have or do live there. Visit historical sites and see if you can feel the spirit of place. You may also want to try some creative methods of connecting with the spirit of place. This could include things like writing, painting, photography or even just spending time in contemplation. Whatever method you choose, remember It is also important to remember that the spirit of place is not something that is separate from us. We are a part of the spirit of place, and it is a part of us.

Spirit Offerings

For many spiritual practitioners, offerings are a vital part of their tradition, whether formal or personal. From honoring ancestors and deities to showing appreciation for nature, offering items is a great way to connect with spirits including the spirit of place.

Offerings can be made in many forms, including food or drinks, physical objects, material gifts or other resources. Some people even offer their time or energy through acts of service. The key is to offer something that is meaningful to you and that you feel will be valuable to the recipient.

When making an offering, it is important to be sincere and respectful. Take your time to choose an appropriate offering and be sure to present it in a way that shows your appreciation. For example, if you are offering food, you may want to cook it yourself or present it in a special way. If you are offering a physical object, you may want to wrap it in pretty fabric or place it on an altar.

It is also important to be mindful of your intention when making an offering. Be clear about what you are asking for or giving thanks for, and work to be clear about the message that you are sending. For example, if you are offering food to your ancestors, express gratitude for their teachings and ask them to continue supporting you in your life's journey. Offerings are a great way to bond with spirit. They can bring you closer to your ancestors, deities, and nature, or show appreciation for all that you have in life. No matter how you choose to practice, spirit offerings will help deepen your connection with the divine.

Whether you are offering food, items, or something else, it is a powerful way to connect with those who guide and support you in life.

Bottle Trees

Spend any time in the South and you are bound to see a tree with empty blue bottles placed upside down on the limbs and branches. Many Southern folks believe that evil spirits can be caught in glass bottles placed outside and upside down. When the evil spirit goes inside it can't find its way back out. I have also seen metal trees made just for this purpose. Hanging glass bottles in trees to capture the evil spirits is just another southern "somethin'-somethin'" that is hidden magick in plain sight.

Mirrors

Using a mirror for a porch decoration is something primarily found in the South, and it's historically connected to our desire to protect ourselves from evil spirits. Like protecting your home with haint blue, putting a mirror on your porch can prevent the devil from entering your home.

The belief is the devil can only enter at night, and at sunrise must go back to hell. Hang a mirror by the door to protect against him. The Devil is so vain he'll get distracted by his reflection until the sun rises and forget to enter.

Spirit from a Place Working

The next time you take a trip and really enjoy yourself, keep not just the sand in your shoes, but deliberately collect some dirt. Keep it in a beautiful jar, a bowl in the middle of the table, make your own hourglass. Each time you flip the timer, trace your fingers through the bowl, handle the jar, you will remember the great trip.

Make sure you're not manifesting a move because gratitude is the strongest emotion that will bring about unintended consequences, not necessarily unpleasant ones, but maybe you wanted to live in the Catskills and got a great job opportunity in Miami where you left a business card or the one-night-stand from Chicago called you out of the blue and it turns out they haven't stopped thinking about you either.

Spirit of the Root

"Lordy, lawdyyy...how you doin' Witchery!?" her voice boomed to the back of the shop and I almost thought I felt the floor vibrate. To say that she filled the room with her presence would be a total understatement of the effect that she had on folks. Hers was a confidence wrapped in unconditional love that is only found when you truly know yourself.

When you can speak your authentic voice and the shadows, the insecurities of envy, jealousy, and greed have no place in your world, is where she spoke from. She radiated a deep sense of peace, joy and love and filled the corners with it. It is also worth noting that she was a large serious looking black woman that I believe could backhand someone into last week with little effort. She didn't take anyone's shit and was very polite about it. A true Southern lady if there ever was one.

She made me feel special in a way it is hard to put words. I felt when she looked into my eyes, she saw inside me; she saw me for who I really am. And her nod and smile towards me was better than a slow cooked pot of collard greens. To get her approval was an incredibly special blessing for me.

Love magick, that's all she liked to work in. She had quite a reputation in the Lowcountry of South Carolina for bringing folks together and for sometimes breaking up folks. Because like she would say, "sometimes the kindest thing you can say to someone is goodbye".

She would come into the shop once a month or so for supplies for various clients she was doing workings for. I always enjoyed the hour or two I got to spend with her as my herbal conjuring knowledge always increased. She was an encyclopedia of walking magickal tidbits. And the way to get to those tidbits was to have a conversation with her.

Once I figured that out, I always made sure that I had good questions to ask and to lean into whatever she was saying. Inevitably I would end up getting out my journal and scribbling notes down just as fast as I could while at the same time fearful that I might miss one of those mystical tidbits that she was so freely speaking in the moment.

I do remember the one afternoon where she came in looking for some good hyssop and when she picked the jar up and opened the lid, she just started shaking her head and said that this one wasn't good no more. I, of course, dutifully took the jar of herbs into the back and dumped out the quarter or so remaining. I then put in a whole new bag of fresh hyssop into the jar.

When I brought the jar back out front to her where she unscrewed the lid took another sniff and shook her head again and told me that something just wasn't right. I then went back and found a different jar and another batch of hyssop and then I brought that back out to her.

She took another sniff and then nodded her head slowly and said, "that'll do". Working the spirit of the root is serious business. But before you ever work with it, you gotta learn it, you gotta feel it, you got to experience it. And the best way to do that is to spend time in wildwood, walk in nature, grow your own plants and herbs, learn about the natural environment that is around you now.

The spirit of the root is what she passionately talked about. Connecting with the dirt that the plant grows in is the key she would tell me. Now twenty plus years later I hear myself passionately telling the shining new magickal folks that same thing. It is in the dirt and the best place to start is your own backyard.

My small 8-acre farm in the Lowcountry region of South Carolina was my sanctuary and teacher for 19 years. There my gardens evolved into established and well-loved seasons of color, blossoms, and harvest. I grew plants for pleasure, food, and for magick. A rosemary bush grew by the door for protection, cucumbers vines grew alongside marigolds, honeysuckle and wisteria draped a trellis and created energies of contentment when stood under. And then there was that bed of foxgloves. Seemed like if you were feeling down or out of sorts, the foxgloves would magnify it.

One of my dear witchy friends refused to walk by them because as she stated loudly "they ain't nothing but trouble!" When she first came out to the farm, she was enjoying herself right up to the bed of foxgloves in my side garden.

They have a nice size area enjoying the morning sun and afternoon shade. Over the years they had multiplied and spilled over their boundaries. From a distance they are beautiful. Up close their energies lean to a dark nature and an attuned magickal practitioner can feel it.

"I can hear them flowers talking. Sounds like somebody's up to no good." She looked down at the foxglove flowers.

Seems they were quite talkative this afternoon with their blossoms in full bloom for another summer in South Carolina's coastal region.

"Don't listen to that bed of flowers. They like to gossip. Have a habit of listening to everything that folks say near this walkway." I replied to her.

I learned a couple years ago to make sure I don't say much when I'm walking by there. Foxglove tends to bring about the darker nature of things, maybe that is why it is also associated with the Fae (fairies). Always needs to be respected and never sit near them if feeling down or depressed.

It reminds me of the balance that is in the universe. That things are both good and bad, cursed and blessed, and that which harms us also heals us.

We designate memory and physicality (dirt) to our space, this is a place we have created, whether it be where we buried our favorite pet, drove a car for the first time or planted our magickal gardens. We all have sacred and special dirt specifically to us. When we go back through memories we can ground into the land, and we can build new memories through the land. This in itself is a magickal spiritual journey.

Plants in Magick

It is important to remember that we do not use plants in the work we do. We work with them. They are our partners and our allies. When we work with plants, we are working with their spirits creating energetic bonds and relationships.

Magickal herbs are used in numerous ways, burning distinct kinds of sacred herbs, incense, and resins as a manifestation base for spirit evocations, as offerings to the spirits, gods, demons, deities, and other entities.

Use as Offerings

Herbs make convenient offerings for the dead and other spirit folk. You can sprinkle them onto graves, burn them, or place them on an altar and bury when done.

Mix into Graveyard Dirt

If you have a jar of graveyard dirt, you can mix crushed herbs into that dirt to lend that spirit certain magickal properties.

Amplify or Dull Spirit Communication

Herbs can boost your spirit and intuition senses, but they can also dull them when needed. For instance, I once had a spirit reach out to me every time I walked by where I had placed their dirt. When I placed a dish of dried rose petals near the graveyard dirt, the spirit calmed down.

Protect Yourself from Spirits

Many herbs have protective properties that can guard you, your home, or your altar from malicious spirits. Carry them on your person when you visit a graveyard. You can even use some to stop spirits from following you. A common method is throwing salt over your left shoulder.

Burn as Incense

Not only do burnt herbs serve as offerings, but they also have magickal uses. Many plants and herbs can protect the altar, enhance divination, or put you in a trance state. You can also create herbal smoking blends.

Cook into Food

Cakes, bread, and other meals are traditional offerings for the dead.

Make Magickal Inks

Magickal inks made from plants often appear in necromancy and folklore.

Sew into Poppets

Poppets are one method of creating a tag lock to communicate with a particular spirit.

Pour into a Ritual Bath

In working with the dead, ritual baths prepare folks for divination or spirit communication. There are many great recipes for creating this.

Brew as a Tea

Like incense, this tea can become an offering or amplify your psychic abilities.

Infuse into Oils

These magickal oils can boost magickal workings, protect your home, or charge your ritual tools.

Conjuring Herbs Today

I wish I could give you a list of conjuring herbs that all practitioners use, but by now I hope you have come to realize that each practitioner develops their list based on the personal crossroads that we each stand on. The region we live in, the culture we are a part of, and the traditions we embrace determines our personal stories, magick, and the plants we connect with.

What I can do is give you a backdoor pass to explore the plants, herbs, resins and other magickal ingredients that are found in a Lowcountry South Carolina botanica (magick shop) today. Papa Nico at Nico World in Florence, SC has generously allowed me to list most of the items neatly labeled and arranged on the back wall of his shop. He supplies these items because local magickal folks buy and use them. This is the best window into what modern folk magick practitioners in this region are using today.

Papa Nico has wonderful magickal tidbits on all his labels. They are suggestions and not necessarily what an individual practitioner may be using it for in their own workings. Always remember that there are many ways, both dark and light to connect with and use the spirit of the root.

Here are the labels as they are in his store.

- **Abre Camino Chip** – used for clearing away obstacles & road opening. Very good in baths.
- **Abre Camino Herb** – used for clearing away obstacles & road opening. Very good in baths.
- **Alfalfa Herb** – protect yourself from Poverty. Mix with money incense & honey. Burn daily for financial problems.
- **Alfalfa Seed** – a traditional "luck" herb. Use for money drawing with Goldenseal & Patchouli. Add to cooking to ward off disease.
- **Aloe Powder** – to bring peace in the home or business. Place under rug to dispel arguments, take powder and mix it with love oil to anoint your right foot.
- **Angelica Root** – add to bath to remove any hexes, curses, & evil spirts. Sprinkle in all corners of your house.
- **Anise Seed** – burn to increase psychic powers and call good Spirits. Place inside pillow to prevent nightmares.
- **Asafoetida Powder** – burn this with Vertivert Herb to assist in cursing an enemy or in focusing on someone leaving you alone.
- **Basil Powder** – bath for new love life. No evil can stay if sprinkle in house or business. Add into Love Mojo Bag. Add into food.
- **Barberry** – keep your enemies away – to close the path in front of your enemies. Sprinkle in front of your house or business.
- **Bat Heart** – wrap with red ribbon and keep with you for card games & lotteries. Use in mojo bags for protection & finances.

- **Bay Berry** – "Financial Problems" – attracts money and good luck in all endeavors. Add into your mojo bag. Burn with white candle for gambling.
- **Benzoin** – on Fridays burn with cinnamon & copal for better business. Also used to purify a new home.
- **Beth Root** – is a female of John Conquering Root. A root for chewing in order to uncross yourself. Good for gambling, mojo (green) bag. Very powerful in voodoo work.
- **Birch Bark** – use for cleansing & in rituals that signify a new start of any endeavor. Burn to expel evil spirits on the New Moon.
- **Black Salt** – don't get mad, get even! Use to keep away bad neighbors. Sprinkle in their path to make them move out.
- **Black Snake Root** – to soften the heart of a loved one. Restore your sexual potency. Use for any other spell/ working.
- **Blood Root** – blend with Blue stone, sugar & cinnamon. Protect & allow you to live in peace. Keeps Evil away if properly utilized.
- **Blue Vervain** – carry in red flannel bag to attract a lover or new friendships. Add to a Love Bath infusion.
- **Blueberry** – make a tea – add Black Mustard seeds – soak overnight & throw in enemies' path. Good for revenge.
- **Blueing Ball** – add to your bath for financial problems. Add salt, ammonia & Fla. Water. Use to remove negativity.
- **Brimstone Powder** – mix with incense & burn to keep evil spirits away. To break hexes & drive away enemies.
- **Buckeye Root** – carried in your left pocket to bring good luck – rub with gambling oil.
- **Calamus Root** – a powerful controlling root. Add powder to any spell by burning as an incense. Most popular in Vodou for strength.

- **Cascara Sagrada** – "Sacred Bark" brewed into a potent tea and sprinkle around your altar to bring good spirit. Help win court cases.
- **Catnip Herb** – add to love potions to calm down a rocky relationship. Mix with rose petals in a large sachet. Can be used in baths. Drink with honey to calm down your nerves.
- **Cerassie** – tea used for colds, flu, bladder infections & blood cleaner. Add honey only. NOT to be used by Diabetics!
- **Chewing John** – aka Low John the Conqueror. Chew a small piece before court case.
- **Chicory** – burn to place a curse on an enemy. Soak name with warm water. Carry in pocket to remove all obstacles in your path.
- **Cinnamon Stick – from Haiti** – used in money talismans. Pair with tourmaline. Protection-bundle 9 sticks together & hang over door.
- **Cloves Powder** – use to insure your magickal intention or spell work is successful. Burn to stop gossip & attract riches.
- **Comfrey Bark** – "Protection", take bath before going on a trip. Protection against all evil and bad luck. Add other ingredients.
- **Confusion Powder** – use to confuse enemies, create strife, arguments & war between two people.
- **Copal incense** – a "holy" incense. Burn with Benzoin & Cinnamon for business. Can be burned when one is seeking Divine "favors".
- **Coriander Powder** – use in love/lust magick. Add to wine to drink with lover. Helps you find romance.
- **Damnation Powder** – mix with Lucifer incense & burn to bring justice. Write person's name 9 times and twist paper tightly.

- **Damiana Herb** – drink as an aphrodisiac. As a tea stimulates muscular contractions of the genital area. Used as an energy tonic and to remedy sexual and hormonal problems. A "sexually tonic" for women. Good for love and attraction baths.
- **Deer Horn Powder** – sprinkle when entering courtroom to make the judge give leniency.
- **Devil's Shoestring** – a piece of this root carried in the pocket at all times will protect against jinx, bad luck, and poison. Placed in the path of an enemy, he/she will have to face financial ruin. Also good for other purposes.
- **Dill Seed** – use in money & love spells. Carry on person to attract money. Take a dill bath to be irresistible to your lover.
- **Dill weed** – sprinkle on food to stimulate sexual desires. Said to quell hiccups, flatulence & indigestion.
- **Dog (Black) Shit** – use in hexing, cursing, and jinxing. Mix with Goofer Dust to cause death.
- **Dragon Blood** – resin powder. Burn during all spell work for protection. Use for cleansing & exorcism of a space. Burn for (9) nights at midnight near an open window.
- **Eggshell** – used in Santeria spells/workings. It is rubbed on the body for protection before taking ritual bath.
- **Eucalyptus** used in purification of ritual tools & ceremonial spaces. Burn to clear the air after an argument.
- **Fennel Seed** – "Law Stay Away" Brewed into tea and sprinkle in front of your home or business, carry in a blue flannel bag. Use daily.
- **Fenugreek** – a house money herb. Add to mop water to help bring money into home. Combine with Alfalfa to increase strength.
- **Five Finger Grass** – brewed into a tea, add to your spiritual bath to wash away jinx, curses, and bad luck. This herb possesses special occult powers: luck, wisdom, power, blessing.

- **Flax Seed** – a potent weapon used to cause fights between married couples or others. Very powerful when mixed with other ingredients and sprinkled on their doorsteps.
- **Ginger Powder** – used in spells to speed things up or cause plans to come to fruition quickly. Sprinkle in pockets for prosperity.
- **Goofer Dust** – sprinkle on the path of your enemies to cause them much strife (revenge). Mix with black mustard seed.
- **Graveyard Dirt** – use in conjuring evil spirits to do your bidding. Very powerful – use with care.
- **Gravel Root** – cut and sifted.
- **Guardian Spirit** – a very powerful herb to add to bath for removing all jinx & bad luck. (This is a personal herbal blend of Papa Nico's containing 7 herbs. Four of them are burdock, skullcap, angelica, and low john. He says the other 3 ingredients are secret because that is his recipe.)
- **Guinea Pepper** – "Grain of Paradise" for protection against evil spirits and to break up an affair or marriage. Creates much strive in a blissful home. Place behind a picture of St. Peter and St. Michael for luck.
- **Haitian Sea Salt** – add to your spiritual bath or burn with incense for stronger power.
- **Hawthorn** – used in weather working, removing evil spirits & concealing magick. Place in bowl to shield premises from evil.
- **High John Powder** – use in Domination spells to ensure success. Burn to help your plans succeed. Use in bath, mojo bags or candles. Use with High John oil to speed things up.
- **High John Root** – this is the most powerful & blessed herb you can use. Helps remove & conquer all obstacles in your path.

- **Honeysuckle** – love, romance, sexuality. Encourages fidelity in relationships. Burn to attract & maintain passion.
- **Horehound** – use in protection mojo bags. Carry to guard against sorcery and fascination. Scatter on ground during an exorcism.
- **Hyssop** – a powerful Biblical Spiritual herb. Brew into tea & add to bath. Considered to be a Holy Herb.
- **Irish Moss** – "Financial Problems" place under rugs to stop money from leaving the house. Brings good luck.
- **Jamaican Pepper Seeds** – use to banish unfriendly people from your life. Mix with Flax to prevent evil from entering home.
- **Jasmine Flowers** – carry or burn flowers to draw wealth & money. Use in love charms.
- **Jezebel Powder** – used by woman to attract wealthy man. Also helps to increase tips. Curse of Jezebel Ritual to get rid of enemies.
- **Jezebel Root** – to make someone spend money on you. Cover with wax from a green candle & bury in a graveyard. Use with Jezebel oil (women).
- **Juniper Berries** – banishes all things, injurious to good health; attracts good health energies, love and protection.
- **Lemon Balm** – used in Love potions & Aphrodisiacs. Drink as tea to soothe emotional pains.
- **Lemon Grass** – "Finding a New Mate". Add with your love potion to create love between two people.
- **Lavender herb** – to promote peace in the home and stop gossip. Add to bath water for good vibrations. For floor wash add Van Van Water.
- **Licorice Root** – use for magickal protection in mojo bag. Put in doll to bind a person from you. Soothes skin irritations & ulcers.

- **Lodestone** – an old practice among the ancients was to carry a pair, one to repel negative influences and one to attract good luck.
- **Lotus Root** – carry to keep thoughts pleasant and clear. Opens the root chakra. Good to use in love & luck spells.
- **Mandrake Root** – carry in red flannel bag to protect against harm. Use for casting spells. Place root near your money to bring more.
- **Magnet Powder** – "Makes spells/workings more potent" Attracts and increases feelings of love. Sprinkle on body, bath, candle, photo, etc.
- **Magnetic Sand** – silver/gold. Used when dressing candle for wealth/prosperity or protection. Sprinkle small amount on top of glass candle. Gently roll taper candle on small amount.
- **Marigold Herb** – add to your bath to make yourself more attractive & appear younger. Use in magick for legal matters & business.
- **Monkey Shit** – used in Haitian Vodou for revenge and dark magick. Very powerful. Creates strife for an individual.
- **Mugwort** – boil into tea to wash all crystal – burn for gazing crystal. Stuff in pillow for dream connection.
- **Mullein** – very powerful when used as an incense. Stuff in pillow to prevent nightmares. Invoke Spirits–Protection – Keep away Demons.
- **Nettle** – an ancient herb of protection. Sprinkle around house to be safe. Use in doll to send curse or evil back.
- **Nutmeg Powder** – used for Luck, Money, Health, Fidelity. Put in mojo bag for extra strength. Sprinkle on green candles to increase wealth.
- **Nutmeg Whole** – powerful money drawing & lucky charm for gambling. Fill hole with quicksilver. Used in spells/workings for prosperity, luck & success.

- **Orris Powder** – a love powder that attracts the opposite sex. Carry in red flannel bag. Use in ritual work for love.
- **Orris Root** – aka Queen Elizabeth – favorite herb for uses in love and romance. Voodoo Queen Marie Laveau used this in court cases.
- **Passionflower** – for Love & Luck Baths. Add to mojo bags. Good for romance. For extra strength – use with agate stone.
- **Patchouli Herb** – Positive – love potion, mix with orris, rose and orange oil/herb. Negative – use to break up love affair with black candle.
- **Patchouli Roots** – mix with graveyard dirt to break a jinx or return a spell. Place under your mattress with love beans for romance.
- **Penny Royal** – "Marital Problems". To bring peace to the house. Bring lovers together who have quarreled or grown apart. Mixed with Dill Seed.
- **Plantain Herb** – use in a healing bath. Brewed as a tea for Divination and vivid dreams. May slow the growth of Tuberculosis bacteria.
- **Poke Root** – use on a New Moon to break a curse or hex. Add infusion to bath water. Carry to increase courage.
- **Pomegranate** – brings prosperity, protection & fertility. Add dried pieces to spells for conception. Use in charm to attract money.
- **Poppy Seeds** – used for causing confusion in Legal & Court Cases and to delay paperwork. Mix with Black Mustard Seeds and carry in pocket.
- **Red Brick Powder** – sprinkle across doorways to stop evil from entering & ward off curses. Favorite of Marie Laveau
- **Red Clover** – sprinkle around house to remove negative spirits and unwanted ghosts. Used in ritual bath to attract money & prosperity.

- **Rhubarb Root** – use in bath to increase willpower and reduce worry. Known to alleviate stomach problems.
- **Rose petals** – use in Mojo bags for love & romance. Burn for love, romance, happiness, and health in the home.
- **Rosemary Leaf** – for nightmares and memory loss. Burn Rosemary when you have visitors in your home. It also improves memory loss and headaches when drank as a tea. Mix herb with bay leaves, ruda, basil, and lavender to keep away evil spirits.
- **Rue Herb** – another herb very effective in breaking the power of a curse. The power of rue defeats the intentions of others. Carry in red flannel bag for protection.
- **Ruda Incense** – burn daily to protect one from curses set out by others. Carry the herb in a red flannel bag for good luck – also use the soap daily for protection.
- **Salt Peter** – add to any other incense to increase power when calling all spirits. Use in a live one's food to prevent the man from having sex with other females.
- **Sandalwood-India** – used for protection, astral projection, healing rituals & in wish magick. Burn at seances.
- **Sandalwood-Haiti** – burn to exorcise demons & evil ghosts, conjure beneficial spirits. Mix w/Frankincense.
- **Scullcap Herb** – "Stop Infidelity" Place herb into a flannel bag with a pair of lodestones and place inside your mate's pillow.
- **Senna Leaves** – make into a tea and let it cool. Anoint on mate while sleeping to stop infidelity. May also add to food to keep them home. May be used for other rituals.
- **Snakeskin** – used in jinxing and crossings when mixed with Goofer Dust. Very powerful to use in court cases.
- **Spearmint** – mix with Gloria incense and burn in your home to rid of demons, ghosts, or evil spirits.

- **Spikenard** – to make your mate more secure and to keep you mate from wandering or cheating. Make tea & sprinkle on lover's picture.
- **St. John's Wort** – used for protection, health, & happiness. Burn on a Full Moon. Brew and drink tea for menopausal symptoms.
- **Star Anise** – used for psychic development, clairvoyance, protection & money. Add to bath or burn as an incense.
- **Sulfur** – used to prevent or destroy hexes or free one from an enemy's power. Can be used for purification before magickal rituals.
- **Tonka Beans** – add (3) beans into your mojo bag, to make all wishes come true. "Special for Gambling"
- **Valerian Root** – magickal properties of turning anything bad to good. Good for love, harmony & protection.
- **Verbena** – a traditional luck herb. Has the ability to turn bad luck to good. Mix with Sandalwood & burn for jinx removing.
- **Vertivert Herb** – burn to overcome your enemies. Remove curses, jinx, hatred, etc. Use in cologne for good luck.
- **Vertivert Power** – place in cash registers to increase business. Make tea to sprinkle around. Burn to overcome Hexes, Curses, and Enemies.
- **Violet Powder** – sprinkle in corners of house to attract good spirits. Use in love bath. Mix with Fast Luck Powder & rub on hands for gambling.
- **Witch Grass** – grind into a fine powder and sprinkle on a black doll/poppet when you want to curse someone.
- **Yarrow Flowers** – overcome anxiety in any situation. Good for love and Divination. Enchances perceptions. Also used for Exorcism.
- **Yellow Dock Bark** – "Business" Brewed into a tea, mix with Florida Water, Vertivert cologne and honeysuckle oil. Sprinkle in front of your business.

Chapter 3

Crossroads Dirt

Crossroads are magickal. It is a liminal space; an in-between; a place where the veil is often thinnest. While many people think of a crossroads as only the intersection of two roads, crossroads take on a myriad of forms, such as a place where land and water meet like the beach, where a field turns into a forest, or a doorway. Where day turns to night (dusk) and night turns to day (dawn). When we are between places/situations/choices in any form, we are in a crossroads, we are in liminal space.

Crossroads are any place that two different environments meet or intersect but is technically neither extreme. It is almost as if crossroads defy categorization. A doorway is neither in nor out of the home; a crossroads is neither of the roads that intersect at that point. Dusk is neither day nor night but somehow both. It is a powerful liminal space often overlooked in our busy lives.

Boundaries are thin at crossroads, where the unlikely occurs and the unworldly cross over. They are liminal spaces, thresholds, and gateways to other worlds, and where magick has more power. Liminality occurs at boundary times, where two opposing ideals meet, such as sunset where day turns into night. Perhaps the best examples of this are Halloween/ Samhain evening, where summer turns into winter and day turns into night, and the veil between worlds is at its thinnest. The crossroads are a meeting of two directions, where a traveler must make a choice between continuing straight ahead and turning onto a new path directly away from the old one.

The first great gothic cathedrals were built literally at crossroads where land or water routes met. People gravitated near water for survival. They needed it for drinking and farming. There villages, towns, cities grew. Most capital cities in the US terminate near a river, even Santa Fe has a tiny river. Crossroads of water and land contain fertile ground for living.

Spiritual connections at a crossroads exist to help people in their earthly existence connect to that plane in the hereafter. We live in a state of transition, coming from two cells, rapidly dividing until we make a whole body. After birth, we grow until we stop; then we age until we die. To make peace with that, people go to spirituality for peace, tranquility, wisdom while we live on this planet. It makes sense to be in a place of crossroads to discuss the crossroads we face while we live preparing for the crossover when we die.

I learned that crossroads are not only where people coming from South, North, East, and West meet, but they also come together the old and the new, the traditional and the modern, the archaic and the contemporary, the young and the aged, the visible and the invisible, the world of the living and the world of the dead.

Every crossroads implies a cross. The cross is a natural and cosmic symbol. Its horizontal arm and circles the globe and a unifying embrace, its vertical arm speaks of the human potential for transcendence reaching beyond the limits of earth. You might think about the crucifixion of Jesus Christ when you think about the cross. This is symbolic of the transition of life and death, of the reconciliation of fallen man and God, sin nature and God's nature.

It is believed, however, that the Greek word "stauros" refers to crux simplex, meaning a simple stake in the ground with no cross-wood element. Some Christian scholars believe that the cross survived because of pagan influences in Christianity, the cross representing the "T" in Tammuz, an ancient Mesopotamian god. He's also known as Damuzid, the dying and rising god.

Living and dying is the perfect example of how the crossroads is a personal experience. In the crossroads, is the in-between. If you've ever witnessed someone crossover, you would know that the process is transitional. Even though the time it takes to die can vary, the person experiences a "sudden change" when they reach the crossroads. The sudden change can vary from each individual, but hospice workers recognize the signs of the crossroads when they've been reached.

The person is alive, but the breathing is different and changing hour to hour. The way they communicate is different. They might speak but it is hard to understand. It's as if they are speaking while asleep. Each of the senses leave the person; hearing is the last to go. This is the crossroads the body experiences as a person literally crosses over from this world into the next.

When we reach the natural end of our lives, it is referred to as the twilight of our lives. This is because twilight is a crossroads. The sun is setting, day is changing into night. There is a power in it that feels different from a sunrise. Sunsets happen slowly, then all at once. The light changes from the golden hour to the blue hour. If you listen and watch the sunset, you will notice that animals act differently. Birds will stop singing all at once. Crickets will begin to sing. The temperature drops. Then you go into the night.

The thing about crossroads is that you only know them when you come upon them and after you've crossed through them. The middle of the road to one person, is the side of the road to another. Crossroads are special and transitory. It is where nothing is black or white and where up can be down. There is a lot of room for interpretation, so use your instincts. A crossroads is an instinct, a feeling, an interpretation. It is something you experience.

Kairos Time

Kairos is a crossroad in the current of time. If we do not take the offered turning, time will quickly sweep us past it. An opportunity that is here and now and may well pass us by. Pay attention to the moment, use your instincts, act spontaneously.

In the film *My Best Friend's Wedding*, Michael tells Julianne that if you love someone, you say it, right then, aloud, otherwise the moment passes you by. They are on a boat, touring Chicago, while a bridge passes overhead. They get covered in shade as the boat they ride passes under the bridge. blocking out the sun. She repeats the phrase, "Passes you by," and looks away from him as they emerge under the Chicago sun. She knows and we know as the audience that she missed her moment. She did not know while she was in the moment that it was passing until it had. I will tell you a lifehack: it's always passing by!

It is the time to admit that, although we have no idea what we will do next, we do know the direction in which we must go. At Kairos, what may be the hardest thing to realize is that we already have everything we need.

Robert Johnson

"I went down to the crossroad, fell down on my knees. Asked the lord above 'have mercy, save poor Bob, if you please.'"
– Robert Johnson, Cross Road Blues (recorded 1936, released 1937).

Robert Johnson might be considered the best blues guitarist of all time. He certainly has the awards and recognition to prove it. To this day, his music exists in some form on the Billboard List of music. It all started at the crossroads.

In his early twenties, Robert Johnson never reached success at blues bars. Owners would not let him perform and bands didn't want him. The story goes that one night he heard voices or perhaps the voices woke him up. Either way, they encouraged him to take his guitar down to the crossroads at midnight. There the dark man greeted him and offered to tune his guitar. When Robert Johnson played the guitar afterwards, he played better than he had ever played. To continue doing so, all he needed to give was his soul, which he did, to the devil. It makes sense why my grandma recited Psalms while she walked through crossroads.

Robert Johnson recorded an album in 1937 and by the time it hit the airwaves, he was dead. He never lived to see the fame for which he sold his essence. That is the way deals at the crossroads go – never in your favor. Crossroads deal in transitions and gray area. They are not what they seem.

Bob Dylan and Eric Clapton name Robert Johnson as their inspiration. Some believe that without Johnson's contribution that we would never have Rock'n'roll the way that we have it. Along with music, Robert Johnson also started the curse of the 27 club that seems to claim other rock greats, like Jimi Hendrix, Kurt Cobain, and Amy Winehouse.

Global Lore

I've been teaching a crossroads workshop for several years now. When I teach it, I like to use notes from the web article *The Crossroads: A Liminal Setting for Occult and Supernatural Activities* by James Slaven. What we find is that everyone is doing something with crossroads, sometimes eerily similar, all across the world.

South America

The America to the south is as diverse as North America. We have to be careful not to lump all the traditions, beliefs, and peoples into one monolith. The crossroads, nevertheless, have similar traditions across the whole world. Perhaps the same spirit in different forms controls the crossroads. We might never know, and that's part of the fun in the mystery of life.

In Guatemala, the Catholic Church made Saint Maximon out of Mam, an underworld deity commonly depicted at churches as sitting at a crossroads because Mayans used crossroads as a place of sacrifice. They built altars here where gods and goddesses would gather to accept the sacrifices and other sacred offerings.

Ixpuztec, the Mayan goddess of suicides, attacked those who wanted to join her in the underworld at crossroads. She exists with a mix of lupine lore in Brazil. Guess when you meet her? That's right – after midnight.

Two other crossroads deities exist in Brazil, Exu and Mula-Sem-Cabeca. Exu rules midnight and graveyards as the lord of the crossroads. He's the image of death in Umbanda, a religion in Brazil. Mula-Sem-Cabeca transforms from woman into a headless fire-spewing mule at the crossroads before galloping through the countryside setting fire to everything.

The soucouyant appears in the Caribbean as an old woman who strips off her wrinkled skin at night and tears across the night sky as a fireball looking for victims. The only way to protect yourself involves surrounding your home with white rice or making a ring of rice at the crossroads. She must pick up every grain of rice before she can cross. By that time, it's morning. She's been up all night. The sun's out, doing her job, why compete?

British Isles

The British Isles contain many different people with many different traditions. It's arguable that Britain did a better job of assimilating everyone into one people. Tell that to the Irish or the Welsh or the Scots. But there exist a variety of crossroad traditions across the empire.

The people erected stones at crossroads to trap beings that should stay underground, like Cnarig Bwt who ate the brains of children. Stones kept the fae out. The stones are also believed to be the frozen digits of trolls and giants who, perhaps, were not so good at keeping away from the fae.

Welsh tradition believes that spirits of the dead (on Halloween) and fae dogs inhabit every crossroad. If you come across one of the dogs, you must avoid or run away from the dog before it barks three times. If you hear the third bark, you will soon die.

A friend of mine's grandfather saw a large black dog in the weeks before his death after a long illness. In Wales, they call him the gwyllgi, haunting "lonely roads", preferring crossroads. Also, a sign of death in Wales, the Gwrach y Rhibyn, similar to a banshee, cries out at those about to die. You find her at your bedroom window at night or a crossroads.

On the Isle of Man, evil spirits and bad luck could be swept away by sweeping a crossroads clean at midnight (which, by the way, is another liminal time – the border of one day to the next, just like sundown).

The Irish and English practiced burying the unbaptized dead, the suicides, or otherwise unholy at crossroads. They believed that this would confuse the spirit, keeping it from wreaking havoc on the living in vengeance for a bad life. The spirits might otherwise inhabit holy cemeteries, haunting them at night. If they were to become undead, burying them in a crossroads would keep them at bay from returning to town. They might take the wrong way. The English eventually put the gallows at crossroads just to make sure all the badness stayed put at the crossroads.

Europe

Like the Irish and English, early Europeans buried criminals and suicide deaths at crossroads to confuse the spirits, preventing them from returning with their bad omen.

At crossroads, Europeans believed that you could bring a dead hen several nights in a row until a magickal black cat showed itself. If you trapped it, brought it home, and fed it well, it would become tame and provide silver coins. If it ran away, you'd have bad luck.

The Gaulic and pan-Celtic goddess of equine, Epona, reveals herself to those who beckon her at the crossroads if she deems you worthy. Modern times depict her as a dark woman on a white horse.

Der Teufel at the crossroads in Germanic lands offers your heart's desire for temporary servitude. He's a monster, and the legend changed to exchanging your soul in permanent servitude. When people converted from the old religion to Christianity, Der Teufel become Satan. At these crossroads is where witches met, and the ritual of cracking whips became common at intersections to scare away witches.

In Roman times, Lares and (in Greece) Hermes and later Hecate, became guardians of crossroads, families, fertility, and cities. Most important for modern Witches and pagan folk is Hecate, the Greek Goddess of Witchcraft. She provides guidance in life choices but can point you in the wrong direction. Remember, advice from the crossroads comes at a cost.

Asia

Lu Tou is the god of the crossroads in China. People leave food to appease him. Or they use torches to shout him away.

The Japanese have Sarutahiko Okami and Chimata-No-Kami. The former is depicted as either a monkey or a man with a long nose, representing male sexuality. The latter is also a phallic god for male sexuality. Some believe that there is a connection between masculine fertility and the crossroads. The number of children a man has is often seen as a status of manhood. Jizo is the god of travelers and family where statues of him have been erected at crossroads.

India

Older than Shiva, Bhairava is God of crossroads in India. Indians are polymorphic monotheists, so they might prefer different gods, but they believe that there is only one god who takes many forms. Families tend to have their own god, considered to be the patron of the house.

Africa

From the African tradition we get Papa Legba, made famous in *American Horror Story: Coven,* but he came to the West as a guardian through the enslaved on the ships in the Middle Passage slave trade. He survives in Voodoo traditions in New Orleans and other places, but most prominently in Hoodoo, where African religious traditions mixed with Christianity.

In Hoodoo, the magick at the crossroads is deemed more powerful. The crossroads is where one goes to make a deal and/ or learn a skill. When you go there to practice, a large black man comes to help. By black, I mean, black, all black, as black as night. I am not referring to race or skin color. Like Robert Johnson and the blues, you will become adept, but think about what you are willing to pay.

Robert Johnson became the greatest blues guitarist of all time. He received a lifetime achievement award Grammy in the 2000's, but he had been dead for nearly 80 years. He never heard his songs on the radio.

Crossroads and Witches

Many stories come together in countless folk tales and modern films, to show how Witches are supposed to covertly meet at crossroads to conduct coven work. The Evil Queen in *Snow White and The Seven Dwarves,* tempts her victim at an open window. A crossroads, no doubt. She offers a poisoned apple, poisoned with magick, in a disguise made with magick, neither inside of the house nor completely outside of the house.

Accompanying her, instead of a black dog, two vultures, excited at the death of Snow White. Like all crossroads, one does not always get what one wants. The Evil Queen escapes from the mob of dwarves to find herself at another crossroads, the edge of a cliff, along with the two vultures perched on a branch, waiting this time, for her fall.

The Evil Queen killed the fairest in the land, leaving her to be the most beautiful. She never got to experience being number one because she had not recovered her true form before she fell off the cliff. Surely, as a hag, she was far from the number two spot of the fairest in the land.

The Evil Queen and her vultures mirrors the association between Witches and Hecate, a Greek goddess of sorcery and magick, who was said to appear at earthly crossroads with baying black dogs at her side. Most Witches, like many spiritual practitioners, understand that crossroads are a vortex for spiritual energy – it is an "X marks the spot" for limitless spiritual and energetic potential. This is incredibly attractive for the magickally minded because the crossroads is a liminal space full of power and possibilities.

In Dreams

Dreaming of crossroads are often symbolic of confusion, and not being able to see our way clear to gain a solution to a problem. It may also be a herald of many opportunities that are in store for us. The meaning of crossroads in dreams are often about choosing a path that honors who we are and avoiding choices that lead us down paths that become dead end roads in life.

Ley Lines

Ley lines are invisible energy lines that lace the entire earth. Along ley lines are often important national and historic monuments. Where ley lines cross, there appears to be a notable uptick in supernatural occurrences. Intersecting ley lines are reported to produce high energetic vibrations from the earth and its atmosphere. These high voltage spots are often blamed for car accidents at intersections, unexplained phenomenon at crossroads, and intense supernatural activity.

You know what else exists upon ley lines? Crossroads. Human activity quite frequently situates crossroads on natural ley lines. Crossroads are considered significant markers for supernatural or spiritual activity. In other words, there are tons of reports and legends about ghost-sightings and spiritual phenomenon taking place at crossroads. Perhaps ley lines are the scientific explanation for that.

Modern Magick

The rituals and magick performed at crossroads can be divided into two types:

1) activities in which an individual sought help or protection.
2) activities in which the liminal point was utilized; a portal of types.

As mentioned in the introduction, crossroads are technically not either extreme, which led to many associating special traits with these places. Furthermore, crossroads were viewed as the beginning of something, such as a journey that often begins by leaving through a door. Because it was associated with the beginning of a journey, protection rituals were largely performed at crossroads to protect travelers in ancient times.

Wax figures (poppets) were often left at crossroads to perform different magicks, mostly love workings. Other manuscripts mention writing an incantation on a three-cornered sherd acquired at the crossroads then hiding it there again. The belief was that the spirits that resided in these liminal places would assist with the desired working.

Other known workings include women in labor wearing an amulet that contained herbs grown at a crossroads and burying frogs there as a precaution against fever. Crossroads, likely because waste was often disposed of there, was associated with disease, so making an offering to the spirits of crossroads was believed to prevent such diseases.

No matter where we look in the world, crossroads have deep magickal roots and have long been viewed as liminal places. Crossroads still play a prominent role in many magickal traditions, including Hoodoo, Conjure, traditional Witchcraft, and most American folk magick practices. Often, magickal remnants are left at the crossroads. It is considered an impartial way to dispose of working remains, such as left-over candle wax, ashes, and even ritual bathwater. While this is a fairly common practice, be aware of the nature of the remains you may wish to leave there. Please be mindful of littering and the potential ecological effects your working's remains may have on the environment.

In magickal workings, the crossroads is utilized as a liminal space to travel to the Otherworld and communicate with spirits. It is a wonderful place to collaborate with local spirits, gain insight and wisdom, and bring depth to your personal magick practice.

Purposes for Crossroads Magick

Crossroads dirt can be used to make magickal deals and petitions but be incredibly careful what you wish for with this form of magick. Crossroads can be a place without time; a friend of a friend's husband got caught in a vortex in Sonoma, Arizona. They saw him driving his truck around for 30 minutes because he couldn't find the exit. Crossroads is where people go to make deals with the Devil/Dark Man and work with malevolent energies.

There are numerous ways you can use the crossroads in your own practice, from communing with deities to working with spirits. These liminal spaces offer so many excellent opportunities for magick. However, be mindful that crossroads are not just physical places, but times as well, such as the Dark Moon, dusk, dawn, solstices, and equinoxes.

Use these places and times to seek protection, commune with spirits, honor your ancestors, leave offerings for a deity, remove a blockage, dispose of magickal remains, banish negativity, set goals, seek guidance, gain wisdom, acquire a talent or any other magick you deem appropriate to be worked in a liminal space.

Magick involving crossroads can be for different purposes, but mostly to bring something towards you or to send something away. At a crossroads, people and things are moving away or are coming near. They are not stationary. That is the power behind the magick.

Crossroads magick can be done to remove blockages that may be preventing you from manifesting something and to remove any barriers. Blockages have no place at the crossroads. They are too busy with comings and goings.

So liminal are the Crossroads that they can be worked to bring prosperity and abundance, working with spirits and spirit communication, honoring the dead, banishing, domination, making wishes, finding direction, making decisions or choices, or when faced with a crossroad in your life.

Crossroads magick can either be done at a crossroad or you can bring the crossroad home by collecting some dirt from a crossroad. Crossroads dirt in workings can be used for purposes that relate to crossroads magick. Just remember that crossroads dirt magick has different qualities depending on the time that you do the magick, even if you have brought the dirt home.

Words of the Crossroads

Symbolic meanings and associations when using words to define the meaning of crossroads:

Balance
Mystery
Decision
Enigmatic
Confusion
Sacred
Possibilities
Equilibrium
Magick
Navigation
Unknown
Acceptance
Repentance
Opportunity
Redemption
Choice
Conscience

Meaning of Crossroads and Life-Lessons

From the cultural and mythological back-story about the meaning of crossroads, we quickly realize that it is a lot about a very localized space in time, place and mind that is brimming with possibility. I recall a story of a Christian mystic or folk magick practitioner, a friend told me.

At the Hardee's in Columbia, South Carolina, at the intersection of I-20 and Highway 321, he watched an elderly black man walk to the side of the road and hold up a bottle of Aquafina water. For thirty minutes, the old man turned in a slow circle shouting, "Thank you Father God, thank you Holy Spirit, thank you my Lord and Savior Jesus Christ." The man held up both arms, kept his eyes closed, and faced the early afternoon sun. Revolving slowly for all the traffic to see.

Before my friend and his roommate finished lunch, the old man unscrewed the top from the bottle and poured the water out in a circle where he stood. My friend decided to stand in the circle when the man had finished his ritual and left. My friend was not particularly reverent. He said a curse word as a joke.

Both my friend and his roommate experienced separate, unrelated medical scares a brief time later. I will happily report that they both came through it OK. According to my friend he had a deep compelling feeling that all was not well and sought medical treatment. He credits the circle at the crossroads for his miracle.

Ultimately, the symbolic meaning of crossroads deals with choice, consequence, selecting the direction in which we want to go. Moreover, standing at the center of a crossroads affirms of being poised in a position of pure potential. When we are suspended upon that vortex of power, the wise practitioner asks the question: "In what direction shall I navigate that power?"

For many of us, being in a position of power requires taking a stand for what we believe, even when we do not know what we will encounter upon the road we have chosen. To connect to the crossroads on this depth it can be helpful to think of the symbolic meaning of crossroads in terms of the equal-armed cross. Create a mental picture of four in-roads leading to your heart with each way representing "highest nature of self":

Spirit
Self
Nature
Knowledge

Combining of these four sacred concepts (Spirit, Self, Nature, Knowledge) we meet life in the middle – the center – which is both the beginning and ending. Also, by utilizing these four touchstones, we create balance and harmony. Through this connection to the power that the crossroads can create, the wisdom of the universe can flow through you creating a soul-quaking, paradigm shifting awareness.

This higher self is the part of one's consciousness that contains the 'Atma', the breath of Divinity individualized as Soul or Self. This Self is completely at one with Divinity. It is the consciousness of being not only a part of Divinity, but of being fused in substance and essence with Divinity as a totality.

The meaning of crossroads is all about liminal space. Liminal is that in-between point that means both we are neither here, nor there. Liminal space as represented by crossroads points to 100% potential and opportunity. It is the place where magick happens because it is that slight crack when/where anything can happen.

Crossroads Dirt

Dirt from the crossroads is different than being at a crossroads to do crossroads magick but you need to consider "what it is" or "who it is" you want to call up or upon when you are doing magickal workings with the dirt collected from these areas. Crossroads dirt is often used in workings for needing to change the luck or direction of a circumstance. It is used in road opening work and matters of advancement in employment.

Its use is probably the most diverse magickal ingredient that you can have in your arsenal. You can use it to cross someone up, to remove energies, or a person from your life, use it in love work to change the direction that the relationship is headed, open new opportunities at the workplace, use as a general location to disperse energies into the universe.

A crossroads is any place where two roads intersect. Crossroads are the place where the world of man and the realm of spirit meet. Therefore, they belong to everyone and no one. Some folks divide crossroads into two types: male and female. Male crossroads are the three-way crossroads that form a capital T; the three points representing the penis and testicles. Female crossroads are the typical four-way crossroads which are said to represent the inner and outer lips of the vagina.

Crossroads signify a convergence of energies and open possibilities, destiny, and transformation. The crossroads are known throughout history as a point in everyone's life that we must make a choice or a decision, yet if we make the choice, it can alter our lives and our futures dramatically. We may wonder later if we made the right choice or even if happy with our choice, we may wonder what could have happened.

Sometimes there can be barriers or blockages that prevent us from receiving abundance and prosperity, other times we need to turn in a new direction when faced with an option or choice. The crossroads is representative of what many of us face and sometimes, it leaves us standing in between this world and the next with possibilities ahead us in different directions.

Types of Crossroads
3 Way Crossroads
This is good dirt to be used to affect a man's gallivanting or wandering eye (and other body parts). Keeping the dog on the porch, so to speak. Take a handful of the dirt and add a representative or items of the man and place in small bag. Speak words of "staying home", "not wandering", etc. Hide the bag in a place as close to center of home as you can get. Consider putting it under the house or in the attic if you have access to it.

Dirt collected from a 3-way crossroads is often used for devotional purposes and divination. Really it is about finding the "right" 3-way. The one that makes you feel tingly (in a good way). I have used it to help open roads and blocked pathways, as well.

3-way Forest
To call upon the local spirits of place/land when seeking an alternative other than the two represented. When seeking to find a choice or option that you need revealed to you.

4-way Crossroads
For Road Opening work, which is to break down barriers and see one's path clear, or to affect a woman's sexuality. If your needs require a bit of darker shadow or more obscure deities, gather your dirt from an abandoned or rural area 4-way crossroads. The spirits that dwell within this area are much more powerful and much darker. This soil is for major life changes, as well as potent healing. It is good dirt to use when trying to overcome something very difficult in your life.

4-way Forest
Use this dirt to call upon feminine energies and powers. Excellent for women business owners to have a pinch or two in their corners.

7-way Crossroads
Major Road Opening work. When you have a larger-than-life obstacle, use this dirt in your working to help open a way.

Seven sequential 3-way crossroads
same as above only ramped up. Take a pinch from each crossroad and combine for an extremely powerful ingredient in your working.

Seven sequential 4-way crossroads
Same as above only ramped up. There are many well documented historical workings where dirt from either a 3-way or 4-way Crossroads gathered at either Midnight, Sunrise, Noon and Sunset are involved depending upon the intention one is

working. So, the time that you collect the Crossroads Dirt may also be important to you.

It is ideal to get dirt from a three-or four-way crossroad that is out of your town or city in an area that is not well populated or traveled often. If you are searching for disused crossroads, consider going to ghost towns, abandoned housing complexes with roads, old logging roads, and country paths.

Collecting Crossroad Dirt

According to many folk magick traditions, when acquiring crossroads dirt, it is expected to leave behind something such as three coins (pennies or higher denomination) at each corner of the crossroads. This is often referred to as "paying for the dirt."

Collect the dirt from each corner or side of the intersection (three side if a three-way crossroad, four if a four-way crossroad) and place in a jar with a lid. Leave the coins on the ground where you collected the dirt at each corner/side of the crossroads. This tradition of "leaving something behind in return" is customary in many folk magick traditions such as when collecting natural items in nature to leave something behind for the nature spirits, faeries, trees, and other otherworldly folks, and thanking them for the item.

Obtaining crossroads dirt may be a little challenging if looking for a particular type of crossroads. Certain workings require the use of abandoned crossroads because the spirits travel there more than they do in hectic highways. Or if you are wanting cemetery crossroad dirt or wanting a series of crossroads you may have to take the time for some serious planning and preparations.

If you are trying to gather dirt or work at an active crossroads, do not walk into the middle, you do not want to get run over by a distracted driver. Offerings to the crossroads and the gathering of crossroads dirt should be off to the side in a discreet area and not in the middle.

Now remember other things like nails, wood, pebbles etc. from these locations will also have some significance but it also depends on what it is and how you utilize it in your workings.

Crossroads always signify choice. Choices can be scary, but they are also liberating. The funny thing about crossroads is they represent both all things unknown and 100% pure potential.

Creating Your Personal Crossroads

- To create a sacred and protected space to do magick in and commune with the spirit realm.
- Can be performed anywhere, at any time.
- To open the portal to other worldly realms.
- To communicate with Divinity or Spirit.
- To create a sacred place for divination.

Petition the Crossroads

To make a crossroads petition you'll want to collect a little dirt from each corner of the crossroads and leave an offering (three blessed pennies in each corner is common) as payment for the dirt. Return with the dirt back to your space. Write your petition on a slip of paper and burn the petition to ash. Mix the ash with the crossroads dirt. Anoint a small taper candle with your preferred oil and sit it in the center of your dirt. Say your petition aloud. Light the candle and let it burn all the way down.

You can repeat your petition as a mantra out loud to heighten your magickal energies. Repeat the request aloud, saying it over and over, building energy around your intention. Shout it to the roof tops if you feel so inclined. Once the candle has gone out, gather up the dirt and any candle wax that is leftover. Add three pennies and go back to the crossroads. State your petition and as you do so throw everything into the center of the crossroads.

This is a remarkably effective form of magick and not to be taken lightly.

Tarot & Crossroads

Tarot has always been a divination tool to look at different scenarios and possibilities in a situation. Divination workings with crossroads magick can open new possibilities and options that can become available and can lead to looking into other directions that you may want to take. This could be your spiritual, career, love, or life path that you may be working on.

If you are at a crossroad point in your life, tarot can help look at the different paths to give insight into each direction and option. Use the tarot cards to help you weigh the situation and make the choice yourself on which direction to take.

Crossroads Tarot Spread

This spread can be altered anyway you like. Take the information and ideas about the crossroads and produce a new tarot spread if you are so inclined or add to the one that I created.

Lay four cards on cardinal points (East, South, West and North). Envision the crossroads and you standing center, now lay the 5th card center to symbolize you standing in the center of that crossroads.

The cardinal point cards represent:

East – New or unknown opportunities or people
South – What needs to be left behind
West – Your blockages
North – What needs to be embraced

4 Lanterns To Open The Crossroads Ritual
You will need:

4 lanterns (candles),

Candle (s) to represent Divinity as you know it
Plate of food offerings
Tokens of honor and reverence (rum, cigars, food, song, coins)
Blessed dirt (3 cups cornmeal, 1 cup ash from a full moon fire and a handful of graveyard dirt)

Place all items center, either on a small table or a cloth on the ground. Start by taking several deep cleansing breaths and focus on your intention for this ritual. You are opening the crossroads for a magickal or spiritual experience. Take each step mindfully.

Move away from the center and start by asking the Gatekeeper permission to enter this liminal space.

Keeper of the Crossroads,
Known of many names,
Here is my token.
Open the crossroads,
Open fate.
Words of reverence have been said.
From my hand to my heart, to my head.
Open the crossroads
Open fate.

Place a token on ground in front of you and wait. Listen to the world around you. When you feel a breeze upon your cheek, a feeling that it is "okay," it is time to continue. If for any reason it does not feel right, then do NOT proceed. Simply pick up your things and leave. Today for whatever reason is not the right time and that is okay.

Now, once you have the Gatekeeper's permission it is time to proceed. From the center start drawing a line on the ground using the blessed dirt. I suggest a baggie with the corner clipped for doing this. Think of it like a cake icing bag. At the end of the line, draw two diagonal lines creating a point, like an arrow. Stand at the end of the arrow and light a lantern while saying:

I call spirits, ancestors, and wise magick folk of old,
Come aid me and tell me secrets untold.
Entrance to those who bid me well this eve.
Here are offerings for you to receive.
A bright lantern lights the way.
Come for as long as you wish to stay.
Amen
Blessed Be
So Mote It Be

Repeat this with the other three directions creating an equal arm cross on the ground using the blessed dirt. Draw or create any additional sigils and symbols on the ground in the space that are personal to you.

Now go to the center and light your candle (s) to Divinity while saying:

To All that is Divine,
In every form, every space and in all time,
Your Beauty reigns in both the dark and the light.
Join me and bless this night.
Amen
Blessed Be

Now is the time to do your workings, say prayers of gratitude, do some divination (tarot, oracle, scrying, etc.) or maybe journal. When you are done and ready to close the space, extinguish the lanterns, take a broom, and sweep any trace of blessed dirt away. While doing this say a heartfelt thank-you for having this experience and opportunity. Use words you feel are appropriate in the moment.

Crossroads Working for Prosperity

The Chinese often use red envelops filled with cash as a wedding present. Red looks strong and fierce, a power color. When a man wears a red tie, he wears a power tie. The next time you watch a presidential debate notice which candidates wear power ties.

Harness the fiery energy of red using your own red envelop, including the best dirt for your purposes, and write the famous Abraham Hicks mantra "Everything always works out for me" on a piece of red paper or white paper with red ink 4 or 5 times but no more than that. Do you want a fast, chaotic prosperity or a slow, thoughtful, deliberate prosperity?

A Spell to Forget

Fill a mason jar with the best dirt for your purposes. Put in a patch of your ex's clothing, a photo of an old friend, or write a poem about whatever you wish to forget. This will be ceremonial, so light a candle, play your favorite song, dance with yourself, make something sweet that you like. When your night is coming to an end, dribble in some wax, add crumbs from what you bake, carry around the jar. Tie beautiful ribbon around the top, like a present. Give it the love you wish you could give to the person or situation you wish you could forget. Forgive it.

Whatever you feel you lost, whatever you feel you are owed, whether it is five dollars, an unfulfilled promise, or an apology, decide that the person no longer owes you. You tell them not to worry about it. Give your love and compassion to the jar, let it sit overnight. Sleep well. The next day, place the jar in an ocean, river, creek, stream, on a park bench, gently in the garbage, donate it to Goodwill, leave it at a coffeeshop, let it steer its own course from now on because you leave what you cannot change in the past.

Banishing Working

Write a person's name in black ink on a piece of white paper. Burn the paper to ashes. Put the ashes and the dirt in a container, like a mason jar. Spit in the container. Saliva serves as a bodily fluid of crossroads because someone can accidentally spit on you when they are laughing, or they can intentionally spit on you when they are screaming.

Spitting on someone is assault, but the saliva shared during kissing is romantic. Take away the niceties, banish them, spit on the dirt. Go to railroad tracks and throw the jar on them, breaking it. Don't do it while a train is coming, and make sure to wear sunglasses to protect your eyes in case shards fly astray. You might also want to put the jar in a reusable bag and sling it on the tracks and throw the whole thing away afterwards. If looking to go a little darker, consider leaving it unbroken, on the track, awaiting its fate, which will be pure banishment.

Chapter 4

Graveyard Dirt

From Egyptian mysticism to traditional witchcraft and folk magick, to the practice of Vodou in the Caribbean, this mysterious and useful magickal tool makes an appearance in spells, incantations, and workings from around the world. Time and time again when you hear the words graveyard dirt or cemetery dust, it invokes images of people creeping into a cemetery in the dark of night under a full moon, doing devious deeds to barter their eternal soul to the Devil for some untold power, talent, or wealth. For folks like myself, these words mean something much, much different.

When the Old Sheldon church in Beaufort, SC burned down in the Lowcountry, the powers that be had to put up a fence around the property to prevent folk magick practitioners and others from taking bricks and bags of dirt I visited the area to pay homage to the history that this sacred dirt represents.

The official reason given was "vandalism". The truth? Backyard gossip relayed that a local politician knew that he was being "hoodooed" and was certain that the dirt from the church was being used. So goes the way of the South, polite smiles, and sour jars. I said a prayer, left a small token and took nothing from the church area. So much has been taken from this place it is time to give back.

A structure built in the mid-1700s, burned, and abandoned so long ago that not a single picture of it during its days of use exists. The beautiful ruins of the church stand amongst enchanting oak trees with their branches draped in Spanish moss. The history of this old southern church can be traced back to twenty-six years before the American Revolutionary War (1776).

Some buildings never lose their beauty, even as they lie in ruins. Time seems kinder and gentler to these locations. The Sheldon Church is one of those places; you won't find any elegant stained glass or ornately carved pews here, but you will find a place that's hauntingly beautiful, disregarding time and the elements, one brick at a time.

Old Sheldon Church was originally known as Prince William's Parish Church and was built in the Greek Revival style between 1745 and 1753. It was burned down by the British in 1779 during the Revolutionary War. In 1826, it was rebuilt only to be burned again by General Sherman in February 1865. There are graves scattered throughout the grounds, so, of course, there are spirits.

The most well-known tale features a woman dressed in a simple brown dress, possibly Pilgrim style, standing over an infant's grave. A feeling of deep soul wrenching sorrow reportedly comes over folks who walk near the child's tombstone. The woman's name is Ann Bull Heyward. She also resides in the graveyard.

I made a special point of spending time near her gravesite and speaking soft prayers aloud, hoping my words would bring a small comfort if needed. Some places are to be treasured and protected. They hold the whispers of the dead and keep a much-needed connection. Be mindful in your journeys and remember that there are places we should not take anything from but a beautiful memory and a soothing reminder of the connection that we all have to those who came before us.

Both graveyards and cemeteries are burying grounds for the mortal remains of the deceased. Graveyards are most commonly built on church grounds or with associations to a church. During the 19th century, cemeteries with no association with a church became popular. Cemeteries as memorial parks to the dead became fashionable as a place to spend a quiet Sunday afternoon walking or having a family picnic.

The Victorian era was a time known for embracing spirituality and individuality outside of the church including the advancements of modernization. It was a time of great advancement in so many areas; medicine (vaccines, antibiotics), the manufacturing industry boom and electricity are just to name a few. It was also a time of high infant mortality rates (death under 2 yrs. old), young women dying in childbirth and multiple wars. No wonder the Victorians created these beautiful places with wide alleys, landscaped plantings, and picnic areas. It would appear as if they were seeking connections to loved ones that were cut short in life.

The fear later associated with these places did not exist then. They were seen by the living as the 'home' of loved ones who had crossed the Veil. A late afternoon stroll among the headstones was just taking a walk with Grandma who was now in spirit form, and it was viewed as quite a natural thing.

In Savannah, Georgia, you can't swing a dead cat without it landing on a paved over 200-year-old burial. Full or forgotten tombs of the dead were paved over for expansion of the living in the city. Small church cemeteries and graveyards that were on the edge of a growing population gave way to modern development.

For a city that really isn't that large geographically, Savannah, Georgia, is a large city full of mortal remains. She is, indeed, a perfect example of a distinguished southern lady with all the decorations and beautiful dresses. But it is underneath the skirts that we find a different story. It is no wonder with both the Revolutionary and Civil Wars fought nearby by, and a yellow fever epidemic that killed 1,000 people in one week alone that Savannah is full of the dead.

Many of the beautiful parks that dot the historical area were in fact graveyards for the residents. As the city grew, the markers would be removed. Occasionally the remains would be reinterned, but mostly not. If you walk on some of the streets, you will see pavers with names etched on them denoting someone is or was buried there.

I first visited Savannah around 1987 with a fellow folk practitioner and dead things enthusiast. This was before the movie *Midnight in the Garden of Good and Evil*, that would change the streets of the city forever. Quiet sleepy enclaves gave way to tourist admiring this one-of-a-kind southern example of living oak trees with Spanish moss hanging from the limbs and beautiful foundations seemingly dotted throughout the old town area.

They came because of the movie, the story of high society murder and mayhem, to walk the streets where these grand parties and tragedies took place. Maybe to somehow commune with the dead they now know by name and have an affinity for. Or maybe to meet Minerva? She was the Hoodoo practitioner from the movie.

Interesting side note here: Yes, Minerva is based on a real practitioner, who I am told was far more interesting than portrayed in the movie. No, that is not her real name. I know her grandniece. She lived outside of Charleston, SC, and would come to have lunch at the botanica I worked at. She is friends with the Haitian Vodou Priest, Papa Nico, who owns the shop.

New businesses in Savannah opened to accommodate and profit from this interest in the book/movie. It was amazing to see a sleepy southern city wake up. But there was also the downside. Tacky souvenir shops grew like weeds. Access to small gardens became a ticket purchase, parking issues, tour groups clogging up once serene places...

I could go on and on and I don't want you to not want to ever go there. I have the old timer bias of "remembering when...." And making it sound like everything was fine, but that really isn't true. There wasn't one decent coffee shop when I first went and now there is access to Turkish coffee and the choice of vanilla and hazelnut creams. Savannah is and was a beautiful place of the dead that I typically still visit yearly and complain about the parking because there is no other place like it to commune with the netherworlds.

Overlooking the Wilmington River, filled with red cedars, blazing azaleas, and oaks dripping with Spanish moss, Bonaventure cemetery is still as striking as the first-time naturalist John Muir visited in September 1867. He stated it was one of the most beautiful places to spend an eternity. Over hundred and twenty years later as I stood under a grand oak tree surrounded by hauntingly beautiful effigies of lives lived and the desire to be remembered, I completely embraced his love of this place.

Located 20 minutes from Savannah, it's easy to get swept away in the folklore surrounding Bonaventure and its beauty and intrigue has long captured the imagination of many poets, writers, photographers, and filmmakers. The cemetery didn't become world famous though until it was featured in the novel (and movie) *Midnight in the Garden of Good and Evil*.

Bonaventure Cemetery began as a small family plot on a 600-acre plantation originally owned by John Mullryne and his son-in-law, Josiah Tattnall. Bonaventure remained in the Tattnall family until 1846 (minus 6 years during the Revolutionary War). Savannah hotelier, Peter Wiltberger, bought the property next. A year later, Wiltberger established the Evergreen Cemetery of Bonaventure, incorporating 70 acres of land in the northeast corner of the property. Bonaventure was now a public burial ground and Wiltberger and his wife were among the first people interred at Evergreen. In 1907, the city of Savannah bought Evergreen and renamed it Bonaventure Cemetery. The cemetery was later placed on the National Registry of Historic Places, in 2001.

Before the popular the movie there was already a long history of the unexplained in the cemetery. One of the stories I first heard regarding the cemetery was about the Mercer plot.

I remember hearing tales about the musical success of Johnny Mercer and his intense affair with Judy Garland. Legend has it that it is their love that is the reason why the flowers at the Mercer plot are in bloom all year, the only place in the cemetery that this happens.

By far the most visited grave sites in Bonaventure Cemetery is that of 'Little Gracie'. Her story has captivated visitors to Bonaventure Cemetery for over 100 years. The wrought iron fence surrounding her grave site is often adorned with little gifts left by people who were touched by the story of Little Gracie. After all, she died at a young age and was left behind in Savannah, all alone after her death.

Gracie was the daughter of a hotel manager, popular with everyone in downtown Savannah because she had run of the hotel (a Victorian version of the famous Eloise of the Plaza Hotel in New York City). She died of pneumonia two days before Easter when she was six years old, and her monument is based on a photograph given to a new sculptor in town named John Walz.

But as the popular radio newscaster of the mid-20th century was known to say: And now for the rest of the story. Gracie became more popular in death than she was alive, as her legend grew over time. At some point after her death, it became popular to leave presents/offerings for Gracie at her gravesite, especially around Christmas. Children leave small toys and candy while parents leave a coin or two and ask for protection for their children.

When my granddaughter was born a few years ago in the nearby town of Beaufort, SC, I made a trip to Bonaventure cemetery to visit Gracie. The ornate wrought iron fence around her site had colorful ribbons carefully tied to it. Around the gate, on the ground were various pieces of candys and sweets. I left her a box of crayons and asked that she protect this precious child now in my daughter's care.

It has been reported that Gracie is still seen and heard today, as she visits and plays at the graves of other children. Her laughter is often heard by employees of a bank that sits on the site where the Pulaski Hotel once stood. Visitors and residents alike have reported seeing Gracie playing near the bronze sundial located at Johnson Square in Savannah.

John Hawkes, a world-renowned paleoanthropologist at the University of Wisconsin-Madison recently observed:,

that every culture on earth has Mortuary behavior whether or not their burial practices are related to religion or an afterlife, even non-human social mammals undergo emotional and social changes when they encounter a dead individual... The appearance of Mortuary practices and special behavior around the dead goes back much further in our evolution than any sets of beliefs that exist in the world today.

Spiritual/Magickal Uses

While the term "graveyard dirt" may sound objectionable, many magickal workings, both ancient and modern, call for it. References for its use are found globally. Graveyard Dirt magick exists in many cultures magickal history. Any place that had graves, had folk magick beliefs. And when the culture or society used cremation, there is just as much belief and use of the ash of the deceased.

Graveyard work is a shared concept albeit different methods in every tradition of American Folk magick. Graveyard work is the core of the southern flavors of folk magick known as Hoodoo, Root work, and Conjure. You are "conjuring up" assistance from the Spirits, most commonly an Ancestor or Guide.

Graveyard Dirt has become a misinterpreted and profitable novelty to make money from unsuspecting customers. It appears to be quite trendy right now. Large supply shops are putting labels on containers of "Graveyard Dirt" could be nothing more than dirt scraped up from the other side of the sidewalk. The connection to Spirit is lost in this deal.

There is no authenticity when the dirt has no story, no personal offering to the Spirit Realm, no basis for a connection. This dirt is bad dead and if misrepresented it can become an attraction to negative energies. Not to mention, using this false dirt can be seen as disrespecting the Spirit folks. Best to gather your own, leave the offerings you are compelled to, take a small handful of dirt, and treat with the utmost honor, reverence, and respect. You have been given an immensely powerful gift. Never forget that.

'Grave Dirt' is soil/earth/dirt collected directly from a gravesite. 'Grave Dust' is scraped from the headstone.

Why Use It

Graveyard Dirt is a staple ingredient in many modern folk magick traditions and recipes. When properly acquired, a small bit of Graveyard Dirt can aid you in ancestral and protection workings, banishing spells, and creating poppet/dolls, gaining wisdom and other workings only known to the practitioners themselves.

Graveyard Dirt is a useful addition in any magickal cupboard; for benevolent uses, it may be collected ahead of time and stored. For working after midnight (malicious uses), it is best to wait until the Graveyard Dirt is needed before collecting it. It enhances magick and is a powerful spiritual ingredient to invoke immense force in our magick.

Graveyard Dirt is used:

- To connect and honor the ancestors.
- In cursing and protection magick.
- To connect with the spirit of a one lost (Necromancy).

- For protecting against dangerous spirits.
- With personal items or physical representations placed in a poppet to control the effect on the intended person.
- In mojo/gris gris bags to intensify the magick.

Graveyard Dirt is the key component in a cursing powder called Goofer Dust. Please refer to the section on Goofer Dust for more information. It can also be added to magickal powders and dusts like Hot Foot, Banishing Powder, Crossing Dust, Black Arts Powder, or for any other magickal working that you feel compelled to add it to.

You can add it to your black salt recipe, to make it protective or a cursing formulation. Thus, labels are important. You do not want to sprinkle the wrong dirt in a magickal working. Your blessing and prosperity are now sickness and poverty.

There are many, varied uses for carrying a small bit of Graveyard Dirt with you or for creating a working using Graveyard Dirt in your magick. Graveyard Dirt protection magick works on the idea that the spirit of the deceased will personally protect you. You can choose a potential candidate, a loved one or an unfamiliar person (Spirit) that has the traits and qualities that you are looking for. Or go to the graveyard and let the Spirit pick you (the gravesite you are compelled to take it from).

Graveyard Dirt has different properties depending on whose grave you take the dirt from and for what you intend to use it. Taking Graveyard Dirt from the grave of an ancestor is preferred. If you are unable to do this, then consider using a grave from a carefully thought out alternate one.

In my own magickal practice, I use dirt from my grandmother and mother's graves for protective and grounding work. For protection, I keep a small bit of their dirt on my alter. Each lady's dirt resides in its own separate container. I bound Mom's dirt in a four-by-four white napkin, tied with a red string. Grandma's dirt is in a glass tube. She seems to like it. I haven't gotten complaints so far. It's all I had at the time. You, too, should use what you have in that moment when working your magick. It's all about using what you have and using what you need.

Many times they give me warnings about things I should not do, small warnings, like "Something's up," "Pay attention," because when I feel Grandma around, I know she's looking out for me. Grandma always wanted what was best for me. Having this dirt is a way for me to stay connected to them. They give me wisdom and guidance.

I also have dirt from the entrance of a graveyard on John's Island, South Carolina. It is in honor of Doc Buzzard and the other local black folks who do Hoodoo in this area. I grew up knowing about African American folk magick: Hoodoo. For many decades I studied with more than a few respected practitioners. Through them, I give honor and reverence to this dirt.

While I cannot tell their stories for them, I can respect them and acknowledge their contribution to this funky gumbo we call American folk magick. Sometimes we are given a window to look through and other times a gate is open, letting someone in. I am honored to have been one of the few given this opportunity to stand just inside the gate. Hoodoo is African American, black folk's magick. Parts of it were/are shared; other parts can't be shared and are closed.

While I keep my sacred dirts separate, I use a pinch of dirt from all of them and combine the pinches in a bowl that I use for cleansings. I like to use this mixture to neutralize or cleanse my spaces and my magickal tools, athame, my garden shears for cutting herbs, or any protection spell I'm working. I have also taken my crystals and put them in the dish of dirt. I sprinkle it on the altar, sprinkle it in the corners of my house.

Whether I lived at the Mason-Dixon line, the deep south, or out west, the dirts I could access, the spiritual folk, and the ley lines I had access to changed. Working what makes sense in one part of the United States might not make sense as much in another region. What if I need a good cursing spell and where I'm at, I don't have the attitude or the materials I usually use for that? My options are that I can do it anyway, I can do it with substitutions, or maybe the magick changes.

Instead of cursing, I can do a blessing. Just as there is a thin line between love and hate, there's also a thing line between blessing and cursing. The southern curse comes to mind: bless your heart. Translation; may your naiveness not be the death of you or may it be the death of you.

Each region in America has its own flavor and all together it creates something that words have a hard time defining. Southern Conjure magick is a blend of influences from around the world. African, Caribbean, Native, Irish, Germanic and/or European folk magick that mixes with what is in that geographic area of that time. Hence the phraseology "funky gumbo."; in reference to the base and that we couldn't have created it without the okra that comes from Africa

For years I really had a challenging time explaining to outsiders what Southern flavors of folk magick were about in a way that was respectful and acknowledging all parties involved. I would use the words Hoodoo and Southern Conjure interchangeably, not grasping both the cultural differences and synchronistic similarities. I have since and continue to learn better and use my words better.

I really believe that as someone of European descent living in America, I have the privilege to not have to think about it. As far as I was concerned everybody was just "doing a little something-something their own way". And the main reason why we don't talk about it is because we don't want anyone influencing our workings.

Cory Hutchenson's book, *New World Witchery; A Trove of North American Folk Magic* academically and historically defines, some of the distinct, and yet synchronistic magickal systems that are present in America. He defined Hoodoo as black American folk magick practiced predominately by Americans of African descendant and Southern Conjure as both black and white folk magick blended with varying infusions of regional cultural and geographical influences.

Reading these academically founded definitions made complete sense to me. It cleared up a lot of trying to use words correctly and explaining to other folks the different flavors of magick that are happening at the same time on the dirt that I'm standing on.

A dirty southern truth we don't talk about in American Folk Magick is the fact that magick was widely shared but also heavily stolen and commercialized for profit by outsiders. I do firmly believe that people love to share but too often with good things comes universal damage. We must all strive to do better and at the very least cite our sources. Give credit where credit is due. Speak their names aloud.

Conjure also means to create something out of nothing. This is the reminder to use what we have and use what we need. Take the everyday normal and see the magick that is within it, looking at the world through magickal eyes. Conjure is about the possibilities once we see the sacredness of the dirt we stand on and yet so much deeper than that.

How To Get it

The name of these places is subjective and personal, whether a cemetery, graveyard or forgotten site... but how we acquire the dirt, what we do to get it and the grave we get it from does greatly matter, because it will become the basis of success or disappointment in individual magickal work. Each magickal practitioner has their own method of collection dependent upon their personal belief, but all those methods adhere to the same basics.

Graveyard Dirt is not that hard to collect but does require some practice and spiritual connection. It can be as simple as finding a graveyard and choosing a grave to collect the dirt from while being respectful and giving offerings. But starting out it could take some time to learn how to connect with the dead. This is crucial as you are thereby honoring the spirit whose grave you have chosen. Consider this as compensation for their working on your behalf.

When we don't compensate the dead for working on our behalf there can be consequences or no results at all. The effect may be as simple as your petition or request neglecting to work. Another effect may be the working backfiring and giving the opposite effect. Yet again it may be as complex as the spirit working actively against you in an assortment of ways, should the spirit decide you were disrespectful or offensive when taking dirt from their place of internment. Anything in between is possible as well, so choose carefully and always be respectful of the deceased.

Be certain to check local ordinances about the best times to visit the graveyard. Some graveyards are closed to the public during certain hours, and it may be hard to explain what you are doing if stopped during off hours by a groundskeeper or night security. If your area in general has laws against digging in cemeteries, you may bring a potted plant or flowers to "plant" as a portion of your offerings. In most areas, no one will think twice if they see someone paying their respects and planting a flower on a grave.

If you are planning to use the Graveyard Dirt for beneficial or protective workings, it is always preferable to choose to use dirt from the grave of a loved one. This may be through ancestral lines, marriage, relationships you define. If you want to use the Graveyard Dirt for malicious reasons or justified vengeance, then you may choose to use the dirt from a loved one's grave who would work on your behalf or the dirt of a stranger's grave with characteristics you desire. If your loved one was very protective, it can aid the working. If using the dirt of a stranger, research the issue, or use your senses and intuition to guide you to the proper grave to meet your needs.

If you plan to use the grave of a stranger, take the time to research if there is a specific stranger's grave that would be best for your purposes. Such as, if avenging yourself for a specific crime committed then find someone who in similar circumstances was triumphant. For a dark and deadly cursing perhaps the dirt from a murderer's grave or maybe a depraved / immoral person. For wanting to gain magickal wisdom then a famous Witch's or folk magick practitioner's grave. In the end it is about selecting specific dirt from a suitable grave depending on the need.

Collecting Graveyard Dirt

The method of collecting graveyard dirt requires some care to avoid disrespecting or provoking the spirits of the dead. Always cleanse yourself at home before going to the graveyard. Take a shower or bath using a good spiritual soap. Dress nicely, you are "goin' vistin'" (said with a deep Southern accent) and should present yourself well.

Before you begin, make certain that you are justified in the use of the Graveyard Dirt. After all, Graveyard Dirt magick is not simply using the dirt; it is used to employ the spirit of the one buried for your intentions. If the working is petty or if the need is frivolous, the spirit may be offended if called to action for such a working. It is best to spend some time talking or communing with them however you feel is appropriate or compelled to. Lay some flowers, tidy round the area, read a Psalm aloud, say a prayer, etc.

Always remember, there is nothing especially odd or disrespectful about planting flowers at a grave site. Just make sure that there are no restrictions about in-ground planting as some cemeteries do forbid this activity. This gives you a sincere justification to dig in the ground and a simple, discreet way to acquire some of the dirt of the chosen burial site. It also satisfies your responsibility to leave an offering or token of respect to the deceased.

Speaking of which; honoring the memory of the occupant is simply common sense. You are asking for their favor. Show some thoughtfulness in return. Appropriate gifts to the dead may include libations of wine or liquor (commonly Rum), cigars, cigarettes (if they smoked them in life), combinations of coins, seashells, or flowers. Items or token of them that a person liked in life may be an offering.

My personal methods are simple and vary according to how I am spiritually led at that moment. I will take time to prepare my plans before going further – that is I make certain my focus is clear. I will do a short meditation about the working and then gather my items in my basket, which may include: a handful of shiny pennies, a few silver coins, some flowers, a small bottle of blessed water or Florida water, a few mini bottles of rum/ whiskey, a sturdy spoon, a white handkerchief to place the dirt in.

Different Various Methods

There are many ways I've heard of people going about the collection of graveyard dirt. Some create an intricate, drawn-out ritual and for others it is a simple procurement of taking a small handful of dirt and leaving a gift or offering. No one can tell you "The right way" to show respect to your ancestors and spirit guides. They are your folks, not anyone else's. Only you know that information. Great grandpa smoked a pipe, aunt's favorite song, granny's favorite desert are your personal connections...

Remember that you are taking a bit of someone's last resting place, to utilize their energy for your magickal working. I personally believe the very least you can do is to ask nicely. And you always leave something when taking something. Granny says that is simply good manners!

That dirt conveys a life and that life's love, anger, happiness, and place in family, community, and society. Never ever forget that. The taking of dirt should always be done in a way of honor, reference, and respect. You should be able to say paying my respects and mean it.

Make clear what you intend to use the dirt for to the spirit of the person in detail so that they know what your purpose is. If they make an objection, you will know. You may feel nauseous, uneasy, or a tingle down the back of your neck or maybe a sudden chill and a cold breeze. You may even hear a "no" in your mind if the spirit is capable of that. These are all ways of telling you they are not willing. If they adversely connect you will need to choose a different grave or leave the site entirely if compelled so.

Also, there are times I don't take any dirts from the graveyard. Instead, I give offerings, thanks and leave the area in a state of gratitude. When we are in a state of giving is when we receive some of the best gifts is my personal belief. I took some fresh apple cider for my grandmother as it was one of her favorite treats. I left three shiny pennies on her gravestone and thanked her for helping to protect us and the great grandchildren she never got to meet.

Examples of Methodologies Used

1. Upon reaching the grave one has been compelled to (intuition), knock on the headstone three times and call out to the spirit of the person interred there. Ask them permission to take the dirt from the grave and then wait for the answer.

If the spirit answered positively then continue by bending over and grabbing a fist full of dirt in one hand from the area located over the heart of the deceased. In the other hand place the gift or offering you brought at the spot where the dirt was taken. Otherwise, the gift should be placed on top of the headstone. Only gather one handful of dirt per visit.

Make sure to bring monetary recompense and gifts for the one whose grave you plan to use. If the person was known to you, bring something you know they would enjoy, flowers, chocolate, a favorite treat, hard liquor, wine, etc. If the person is unknown, use your best judgment. Also, bring coins, typically bringing 13 copper pennies prior to 1982, silver coins, etc. is acceptable for most spirits.

2. Always take your dirt from under the sod or top layer. Remove the sod first and set it aside. This includes any weeds and grass, from the area of the grave where you plan to collect the dirt. Using your hands only, scoop aside the top few inches of dirt, after that you may collect the dirt a few inches down into the grave. Fill a small bag with dirt from the grave. Add your gifts to the hole, then, bury them by refilling the hole with the soil you removed and re-top the area with the clot(s) of sod you removed first.

If you are seeking love or protection, claim the Graveyard Dirt from over the heart area. If you plan to use the Graveyard Dirt to seek wealth, arcane connection to the spirit, or knowledge, take it from the area near the head of the grave. If you plan to use the Graveyard Dirt to bring ill or curse another, take it from the foot area of the grave.

Finally, be certain to thank the spirit for their dirt and for agreeing to work with you in your magickal endeavors. Be specific in how thankful you are for their assistance and let them know that you are honored by their assistance and that you respect them for their assistance.

3. When you reach the gate of the graveyard pour an offering at the entrance (rum is traditional but you can experiment with offerings) and listen for the response of the gatekeeper spirit.

Only proceed if you get a firm yes! If you receive no response or a no, then do not proceed.

If you receive permission to enter spend some time walking amongst the graves, quietly speak with the spirits there and pay your respects. When you choose a grave and gather your dirt then leave either three or nine blessed pennies as payment (you can bless pennies by cleansing them and anointing them with ritual oil or water). You may also wish to leave fruit or bread for the spirit who has allowed you the use of their grave and say a blessing for all the spirits in the graveyard. Then announce your intention to take some of their dirt. Make sure you tell them what it is for, offer payment and thank them for their help.

When to Gather Graveyard Dirt

If you are collecting dirt from an ancestor, go on a time of significance to your chosen ancestor. A birth date or death date might be meaningful, but so might a favorite holiday, season, or marriage anniversary. Connecting with your family's stories and honoring them is an immensely powerful connection. Every Sunday after Easter, my grandma would take the flowers used in the Easter celebration from the church and place them on her families' gravesites in the nearby graveyard. That Sunday is a perfect time for me to put flowers on her grave now.

In many folk magick magickal practices, the full moon is a useful time for collecting ingredients designed to bring things to you. The new moon is useful for sending or banishing things away. All Hallow's Eve, All Saints Day, and All Souls Day are particularly sacrosanct times to visit. Many cemeteries will have a formal blessing or ceremony planned on these three days.

It is important to note any rules in your local cemetery. They are often posted near the gates or in another prominent places. Many cemeteries close at sunset or are only open to the public during certain hours. It also may be best to replan your visit to a small cemetery or grave site if funeral services are in progress.

The traditional time for collecting graveyard dirt is around midnight. This is fine if you are visiting a burial ground out in the country where it is rural and a bit secluded. Be respectful and try not to look questionable. It is also advisable not to go alone, simply for safety's sake. A trustworthy friend is the wise thing to have if you will be in an isolated area. Also, never consider climbing over gates or walls because it can be dangerous, and that can also be considered trespassing. Not only can you be fined, but arrested, charged, and end up with a criminal record.

My typical excursions are to places I am familiar with and during the day when I can walk around largely unnoticed by any staff that may be there. I often will take a picnic basket and blanket; so, I can spend time finding just the right place. Having a nice lunch with the dead is something I highly recommend if you have not already done so.

Now I want you to take a deep breath and exhale because I am going to let you in on something that you have already probably done. Remember when I told you about how towns and cities grow and that sidewalks are now on top of old graves? Well, Savannah, GA, isn't the only city that this happens to. I would imagine that it's probably happens all around the world.

Cemeteries and graveyards gave way to the building and expanding of the living around the globe. In San Diego CA, is a beautiful old cemetery right smack in the middle of Old Town. There you can stroll among the white fences and stone circles laid on top of grave sites. Right beside it is a restaurant and if you look on the pavement you will see little markers that denote the grave sites. On the day that I was visiting, the outdoor area patio was full of diners who were having lunch with the dead; most if not all of them completely blissfully unaware.

Most large cemeteries have business offices where you can get a map of the grounds, point you to the graves of persons of public interest and will often show the original size of the site if it has been altered. Look for a list of rules and the hours the cemetery is open. Smaller graveyards may have a similar pamphlet available from the church admin office.

Since interest in funeral customs and art has increased rapidly in the past few years, no one is going to think twice about you going about your business. It is fairly ordinary to see people leaving small tokens, pebbles, seashells, or coins on graves these days. Remember to use common sense and be discreet in your actions. Work with honor, reverence, and respect and all will be well.

Sometimes I will pay attention to the various magickal times and correspondences according to the type of work I am doing. Full moon, new moon or sunset or sunrise would be the most common times cited in many magickal practitioner's journals. Then at other times I go to the graveyard because it feels right. I will meditate and ask my personal spirit guides in finding the right burial site I need to spend time with.

At the gate of the cemetery, I leave an offering to the Gatekeeper. The gift will depend on what I am compelled to leave. Examples in the past – nine shiny pennies, cigar, rum, seashells. I stand there for a minute or two and without thinking to deeply, I take out of my basket what feels right for this moment, this graveyard, and this Gatekeeper.

There have been times where I have left nothing and just nodded in respect as I walked through the entrance. Sometimes that is all that is needed. Every graveyard and every Gatekeeper are different for me.

Who is the Gatekeeper?

Dark Man

This complex, yet simple entity is a manifestation of "empowerment in the face of the unknown". He is associated with both the graveyard and crossroads in American folk magick. Often referred to as the devil but not in the Christian association but rather the folk magick, funky blending and creation of this entity whose roots may lay in Papa Legba and the Middle Passage.

Papa Legba / Ellegua
He is seen as an opener of crossroads and cemeteries. Variations used throughout the Caribbean, Haiti, and southern parts of North America. His roots are from Africa, where he survived the Middle Passage with his stories, lore and magick being carried by black folks and planted in new dirt because they had no choice. Always address with reverence. Sometimes he may appear as an old man and other times he is young and handsome, but the eyes never change.

Old Man at the Gate
References found in the southern Appalachian Mountains and moving up along to northern pow-pow (Germanic influences) folk practitioners. He appears to be a toll-taker of some type. Like the mythical ferry man who charges a payment of some kind to take you to the other side.

Gatekeeper Spirit – just generalized
There seems to be a consensus among magickal practitioners of all regions that you need to acknowledge the spirit of the gate. For many this is often referred to as the gatekeeper spirit with no further description. I like that. It for each of us to see the gatekeeper that we need to see.

Choosing A Grave
Graveyard Dirt often takes on many of the properties embodied by the person who was buried there. It is always best to do your research and choose the grave you will get your dirt from carefully. Select a grave site with meaning to you and your intention.

For example, if you want to use the dirt for a protection working, the grave of your relative who worked as a police officer or a soldier in life would be a good choice. Graveyard Dirt from the resting place of a successful banker acts well for workings to safeguard your financial assets. Or collect your dirt from the grave of a well-respected judge for justice and fairness in a court matter.

If you maintained a close personal relationship with the deceased in life, it will be easier for you to maintain that relationship in death, either by caring for the site, bringing flowers, or honoring them yearly during the season of the dead (Oct-Nov), or any time you deem important.

The use of Graveyard Dirt in a working is utilizing sympathetic magick, and there are powerful beliefs connected to the role of the dead in rites of invocation for many folks. Again, honor, reverence, and respect will serve you well. I place the flowers or a small token as a way of introducing myself and ask the spirit there if they are willing to assist me in the work.

If I get a positive response and I feel good about our intuitive conversation, I will remove a small piece of the sod, take some of the dirt, put it in my handkerchief and make the proper offering. This act is considered by many to be a payment. My offering may be a combination of coins or whatever items I feel are correct offerings, then I replace the sod.

In the taking of the dirt and making an offering, many practitioners consider this to be purchasing the spirit's services for the work. The spirit has fully consented to this agreement for their services and will assist in the working until it is done, then the spirit will be released and free to go wherever they want or need to.

The spirit is never forced or coerced into doing something to which it does not approve; that would be foolish and dangerous. The purchase and use of graveyard dirt is an act of necromancy.

Once again, it is wise to follow the respected and well-honed practice of not calling up what you cannot put down.

I will make sure to record the name of the dead soul and information found on the headstone or marker on a piece of paper and place it in the handkerchief with the dirt. While there are many preferences as to which part of the grave to take the dirt from, those are individual inclinations. I will take dirt from where it is easiest to remove and replace the sod and soil or where I feel compelled is the right place.

Types of Grave Marker Symbols

The symbolism and icons carved onto the stones can be quite thought provoking and also be an indicator of the time that the person was buried, and characteristics or traits of that person. It is good to know or have a working knowledge of common symbols found on grave markers to help you with determining a grave to give an offering to or when dealing with an unknown gravesite.

Gravestone iconography has changed over the years. Visitors in early American graveyards will observe symbols that remind us of impeding death. The 17th and early 18th centuries were preoccupied with mortality and the fear of dying. The bitter reality of death was portrayed with spent hourglasses, winged skulls, skeletons, scythes, coffins, and candle snuffers.

Attitudes changed in the 19th century. Rural Park cemeteries became popular, and the stones and monuments were covered in floral designs, wing cherubs and angels, weeping willows, draped urns, heavenly gates, lambs, and other gentle symbols to remind us that death would reunite us with our loved ones.

Commonly Found Symbolism

- **Acorn** – the seed of the oak a symbol of strength and potential. And Celtic and Norse culture, acorn symbolize life, fertility, and mortality.

- **Anchor** – symbol of hope, or the seafaring profession.
- **Angel, weeping** – mourning or grief.
- **Arch** – is a victory in death.
- **Arrows** – mortality.
- **Bird** – eternal life.
- **Book** – a scholar, faith, the book of life.
- **Bouquet** – grief, sorrow, condolences.
- **Bridge** – between life and death between heaven and earth, physical and spiritual.
- **Broken column** – life cut short loss of head of family.
- **Broken ring** – family circle severed.
- **Buds** – the spring of one's life. Renewal of life.
- **Bugles** – military or resurrection.
- **Butterfly** – resurrection, transformation, rebirth.
- **Calla Lily** – symbolize this marriage.
- **Candle** – divine light of Christ, truth, eternal life.
- **Candle being snuffed** – mortality, time has run out.
- **Chains** – golden chain bounding the soul to the body, I.O.O.F. (Odd Fellows) insignia.
- **Chalice** – the sacraments, with white circle, Holy Communion.
- **Cherub** – innocence, Angelic.
- **Clock** – time has run out, a new beginning.
- **Corn** – lived to a ripe old age.
- **Coffin** – mortality.
- **Cross** – symbol of faith.
- **Cross, Celtic** – Christian symbol of unification of heaven and earth, Ireland.
- **Crossed swords** – Calvary or military person.
- **Crown** – the crown of righteousness.
- **Crucifix** – the sacrifice Jesus made for human salvation.
- **Daffodil** – death of youth, desire, grace, art, beauty.
- **Daisy** – innocence of a child, purity of thought, Jesus the infant.

- **Dart's** – death, mortality.
- **Dog** – courage, loyalty, vigilance.
- **Door** – passage from one life to another.
- **Dove** – peace, the Holy Spirit.
- **Drapes** – also called a Pall, morning, or mortality.
- **Eagle** – courage, power, victory, and height.
- **Father time** – mortality, death.
- **Flowers** – grief, sorrow, remembrance, condolences
- **Fruit** – abundance seeded fruit symbolizes immortality, life, and potential.
- **Garland's** – victory and death.
- **Grapes** – slash grapevines Christ blood and his sacrifice.
- **Hand with a pointing finger** – looking to God or heaven, gone home.
- **Handshake** – a variety of meanings including friendship, solidarity, unity partnership, greeting or goodbye.
- **Heart** – love of Christ, true bliss.
- **Hourglass** – the swiftness of time, time is running out, the cycles of life and death.
- **Hourglass with wings** – a short life, time flies.
- **Ivy** – faithfulness, immortality, friendship.
- **Lamb** – sacrifice, innocence, purity, gentleness.
- **Lamb** – knowledge, love of learning.
- **Laurel wreath** – victory.
- **Lily** – purity, light, and perfection.
- **Lion** – courage, pride, strength, wisdom, and valor.
- **Oak leaves** – strength, maturity, ripe old age.
- **Pinecone** – fertility and immortality.
- **Poppies** – eternal sleep, rising sun and mortality, resurrection.
- **Rose** – brevity of life, perfection, completion, scales justice and balance, legal profession.
- **Shattered urn** – an old person.
- **Sheaf of wheat** – ripe for harvest.

- **Ships** – seafaring profession, hope.
- **Skeleton** – personification of death.
- **Skull** – mortality, life and thought.
- **Star** – wisdom, divine spirit steps ascension, stages, or levels.
- **Thistles** – Scottish symbol of remembrance.
- **Torch** – upside down torch represents death, an extinguished flame. Right side up is the power of fire and life.
- **Trees** – life and nature.
- **Urn with crepe or wreath** – mourning.
- **Willows** – symbolize sorrow (Weeping Willow).
- **Winged effigy's** – the flight of the soul.
- **Wreaths** – victory and death.
- **Yew leaves** – eternal life.

Graves of the Recently Deceased

Someone recently deceased and buried creates fresh, tilled-up dirt. As fresh as the mourning their friends, family, and communities might experience for the passing. The funeral experience represents the last time we exist on the surface of the world together. A handful of dirt at this time represents that they don't travel alone, that we'll be along soon enough, and we remember where they are.

Unfamiliar Grave Dirt

When you are proposing to take dirt from someone you do not have a connection to, you need to tread carefully. Take the time to read the information on the headstone, meditate for a while and be respectful.

Then, ask if you can please have some dirt, and concentrate on the feeling you get. I usually feel a warm tingle in my fingers and toes which lets me know it is ok to proceed. If you experience any negative feelings, physical or emotional, then it is wise to thank them politely and move on. I would not recommend taking anything, even if you have left an offering when you get a bad sense about the situation. It is not worth the hassle.

The potential problem associated for digging up dirt from an unfamiliar grave could result in blessing instead of cursing, cursing instead of blessing, cursing yourself, and the magick just plain not working. When you take dirt from a grave, you need to know the person inside and out. You need to think about the story that you tell when you use the dirt from the grave.

I'm thinking of the new *Golden Girls* tarot card deck. These powerful ladies are ripe for magick but imagine that you visit your favorite character's grave and don't know the actress's name. You could be using Sophia Italian cursing dirt when you wanted Blanche love magick dirt. What if you used Rose dust when you wanted educated Dorothy dirt for an upcoming exam? You would've just cursed yourself. That's not even taking into consideration an actress that might not want to be associated with the character. Rumor has it that Bea Arthur did not like to interact with the audience. Her dirt might be a hassle.

I might be inclined to use a pendulum to find a grave from which I can dig the dirt. Everyone should be able to recognize their own pendulum's swing for yes, no, or maybe/uncertain. The easiest way to find your momentum relies on testing the pendulum in a neutral space, which means when you're at home, not out in the graveyard, hot and ready to disturb some remains. The point will always be never to disturb the spirits. We respect the dead. We respect the families of the dead.

To test your pendulum, before taking to the graveyard, is simple. Test the words, "yes" and "no." Your pendulum will move one way for yes, and it will change for no. Many people make videos showing how to test their pendulums, involving floating the pendulum over certain fingers, giving positive, negative, neutral readings. In my opinion, these tests are complicated and unnecessary. Who decides the energy a particular finger radiates? Who can remember? It won't read the word "maybe/uncertain." The only way you will know is if you ask it a question in a real-world scenario. If the swing isn't one you recognize as either yes or no, it means that the answer is uncertain. Ask a different way.

With the pendulum, see if you're getting yes or no swings around different graves. Maybe or uncertain swings might be indicative of spending time at the grave. Maybe the spirits have a message. When you're used to using pendulum, you can see if you can interpret the messages. You might try closing your eyes and waiting for message from the beyond. That's if you have the time and the persuasion. On dirt gathering missions, look for strong yesses before going further.

If you're still not certain, find the largest tree in the cemetery or at the east-most point of the cemetery. Treat the tree as you would a grave and honor it appropriately.

Types of Graves

While some graveyards may be segregated, integrated, designated for a particular religion, not all graves will be the same. People live varied lives, they die at different ages, they've fulfilled certain roles in the great plan of the universe. Many people do not realize that not all graveyard dirt is equal. The dirt can be collected from various locations within the cemetery, as well as the gravesites that it can be chosen from. This will have influence in your workings and needs careful consideration.

A working for a reunion might not go as well if you take dirt from a bachelor or a spinster. For a long happy marriage, it might not work well to use dirt from a man married multiple times or to take dirt from one of his many wives' graves. If you're wanting to do an attraction or manifestation working, taking dirt from the town gambler might not work well if he spent his time losing, and if he were a winner, maybe he could handle a certain amount of stress in life that the practitioner might not be comfortable with. These factors play a role in the magick.

For some practitioners there is importance not only in the actual site chosen but also where on the site the dirt is taken from. Common is the belief that when working good take from the right side of the grave and when cursing/hexing taking dirt from the left-hand side. Taking near the head for some workings and near the feet for others is also commonly noted in practitioners' journals. Again, intuition and following what you are compelled to do is the best advice I can give you.

This is by no means a complete list of types of grave dirts and their uses. I have seen other lists with other uses stated for the dirt. I have kept this compilation from sources within the folk magick community and a few practitioners I personally know.

Abused Spirit
Several noted practitioners have stated that the dirt collected from over the heart can be used to endure traumatic events or situations. This is the dirt of survival of coming back with a vengeance. It can help in removing yourself from a seriously dangerous or damaging relationship. The dirt collected from an abused spirit (emotionally or physically abused) is powerful. It brings perseverance, at all costs. Collect from areas you feel compelled to.

Adult
The dirt collected from a mature adult's grave is considered an all-purpose dirt. It can help with wisdom, maturity, day to day events. You should collect this dirt from near the head on the right-hand side.

Baby/Infants
This dirt is used mostly for fertility type workings. For someone wanting to become pregnant, or ending it, depending upon the

circumstances. It also embodies innocence, and peace. Dirt used in a working collected from a baby's grave can create peace within a home or relationship. Collect this dirt from the center of the grave.

Cheating Lover/Partner
This dirt is perfect for issues with a potential third wheel on a two-wheel cart; choosing between two or more lovers. This dirt can also be used to cause a spouse or lover to cheat. Collect this dirt from over the heart. You may choose the dirt from the best grave but think about the implications of the grave. Collection from a civil servant might involve a legal battle you're not prepared for, or you might want to collect it from such a grave to help in the legal battle that you're already participating in with the dissolution or reunion of your relationship. Do you want peace or chaos? What grave will help you achieve your end?

Doctor/Midwife
Understandably, this dirt is perfect for healing matters, as well as treating illnesses. On the other side, it is also employed to cause sickness and illness. Collect this dirt from the right side to heal and from the left side to curse.

Executed/Executioner
Collect this dirt for cursing and hexing, revenge work, anything where imposing harm is the chosen outcome. Acquire this dirt from near the head of the grave or near the hand on the left side of the grave.

Firefighters
This dirt is often used to keep a house or business safe from a fire. These types of folks have a personal stake in protection.

Try to take dirt from near the foot of the grave on the right side (stomp out the fire) to protect. Use left sided dirt from a bad or ineffective firefighter to create a fire (a known arsonist is even better).

Gambler

This dirt is used in mojo hands, dice throwing, anything that can help better the odds and increase luck. This is used for both gamblers and new business owners, equally. This dirt should be taken from near the right hand on the right side. Take from the left side if used to make someone lose a bet, or not be lucky.

Journalists

A handful of this dirt is often helpful for uncovering the truth of things or helping to spread malicious gossip. Take dirt from the head area to find the truth in matters. From the feet area for creating false stories and spreading gossip.

Judge or Lawyer or Law Enforcement officer

Court cases, road opener workings, honey jars, any working where you are seeking justice. It can also be collected from a "dirty" lawyer or a judge that was known to accept bribes. This dirt is used when seeking to corrupt a person. Collect the dirt from the right-hand area of an honest judge/officer for positive workings and the left-hand area of a dirty judge/officer for the darker workings. The right-hand dirt can also be used to keep the matter up front and receiving attention.

Murderer

This dirt is traditionally used in workings to bring harm to those who have harmed you or your loved ones. By collecting this type of dirt from the left-hand area of the gravesite, you can invoke the powers of revenge. This dirt is perfect for harmful or nefarious workings. Be mindful that working with this type of influence can become quite damaging for both the practitioner, as well as those it is for.

Partner (lover, spouse, etc.)

A small handful will aid in bringing a new love to you. If the previous relationship was loving then this will aid in finding a new relationship. Gather dirt from the heart area.

Priest or Clergyman

Collect this dirt from the head of the grave, very near the stone. This dirt is often used for protection, as well as spiritual guidance and understanding. Enlightenment, high powers, divination purposes will benefit from this dirt. Another use is for letting go of painful things.

Pet

If you can collect dirt from a beloved pet, this can be useful in protection, love and understanding. Many feel that this type of dirt is also good for loyalty matters. Collect this dirt from anywhere on the grave.

Sailors

This dirt can be beneficial for long travels or time spent away from home.

Soldier

This dirt is used for courage and bravery, steadfastness, loyalty. Problem solving, thinking outside the box, self-preservation, secrecy, covert operations. This dirt can also be used to control someone else, to cause them to obey orders. Collect this dirt from the right hand, above the heart, or near the head; whichever makes the most sense to you. Write a handwritten letter to them as an offering; mail/letters from home were/are priceless for these folks.

Suicide

Many necromancers choose the dirt from suicide victims. It is often used in very dark magick, jinxing, hexing, driving something far, far away. It can be used to cast torment, anguish, and extreme sorrow. Collect from the feet. Make absolutely sure that you know that this is the right dirt for you and your situation before ever consider even using. These spirits can be extremely difficult to work with. Again, do not call up what you cannot put down.

Wealthy Person

Use dirt from this grave to draw riches to you or take away money from another person. Again, right side dirt to draw towards you and left side dirt to take away money from someone else. Your offering should be something that is golden or represents treasure (be creative!)

Writers/Poets

Have writer's block or feel like there is a story inside you just waiting to get out? A small handful of this dirt in a working is useful for work involving inspiration or creative forces. Leave an offering that you are compelled to. Different writers are different folks, use your best judgement.

Teachers or Educators

Gaining knowledge, passing exams, and assisting with matters of careers may need a little magickal help with the aid to of this dirt. An offering may be a piece of chalk or an apple.

Young Adult

Dirt collected from anywhere on a young adult's grave can be used for a variety of things. Romance, new relationships, sexual attraction, but also irresponsible behaviors, lack of accountability, excessive behaviors (drinking, drugs, etc.). Again, proceed with caution when compelled to use this dirt.

Young Child

Many practitioners deem this very powerful dirt, and it must be treated with the upmost respect. This is the grave of a child. Bring toys and sing fun children's songs as offerings. Use this dirt to help protect other children.

The Intranquil Spirit

This is the name given to a type of dead soul that wanders restlessly but can find no home or resting place, thus the description "Intranquil." The Intranquil Spirit cannot rest in peace and therefore, it is particularly unhappy, angry, and vengeful.

To work with this spirit, collect dirt from a 4-way crossroad in the graveyard. 3 a.m. is said to be the best time to do this.

Other Graveyard Dirts

All dirts have imbued energies in them and are deemed extra powerful when in a graveyard area.

Ant Hill

Ants are small but can lift more than their weight. When a hoard attacks a bug or covers a dead animal, they can carry it to the nest and strip it of nutrients in hours. Dirt from their hill allegedly causes financial discord: Gather dust from an anthill and sprinkle it on your target's property or on them if you can. (But don't put any ants on a person or their things. Some people are allergic. You might be too, and they don't travel well.)

Cemetery Entrance

You know the feeling when you see the cemetery's entrance and then the feelings when you pass through hit? It's foreboding. The dirt collected from the entrance or near the entrance of a cemetery is perfect to use when requiring strong and powerful protection. It provides a strong guardianship. And when sprinkled around the home or business, it will help keep unwelcome spirits away.

Cemetery Center

Graveyards exist within a set number of square feet in space. The power is all around in its designated area. Use a map of the layout of the cemetery or pull up a satellite image on your phone and find the four farthest corners you can safely get to as well as what is the center of the cemetery. Once you find those five points (the corners and the center) put it into a bag or jar for safe keeping. This is used in protection from spirits.

Forgotten Cemetery

Sometimes a cemetery goes out of business, but a city protects it because they can tell that it is a cemetery. In time, the stones will wear away, it will be an ancient burial ground, people will build on top of it. That results in dreadful things sometimes. For now, it is in transition from what it was to the new future. This dirt is highly effective in crossing and hexing workings. May the target be forgotten, lonely, and tormented. You can collect it from the entrance or at the center of its location.

Mole Hill

While we live above ground, moles silently work under our feet. We notice them when we see their mounds. They are bringing slow, silent change. Sometimes they can disrupt concrete on top of them. Gather some dirt from their mounds. Use it to create discord and increase difficulties for someone who has wronged you like the adage "to make a mountain out of a mole hill."

Water Edge

In a dream, two friends of mine in a relationship traveled to the tip of Florida. One said to the other, "So this is what the end looks like?" A few weeks later, they broke-up. Memes say that what cures heartache is salt water, whether sweat, tears, or the sea. So, too can dirt near the water break-up a marriage or relationship; this is especially good if the relationship or marriage is abusive. (This is for Graveyards that bank up to the edge of a river, stream, or ocean)

Votary Cross

This is the symbol of the sufferer. Dirt collected from this is used in rituals to reject suffering. To be likened to a ship which navigates the sea of suffering the greater the hardships befalling him, the greater the delight he feels, because of his strong faith, usually from a grave of a devoted (almost religiously so) adherent of a cause, some people would substitute the word "Martyr" or "Saint".

Memorial Stone Dirt

Sometimes a body is not recovered or is otherwise disposed using cremation. Families still place a marker because it is nice to have someplace to go. I have used dirt from such a grave if you can call it a grave. Some practitioners swear that they would never use dirt from these places because the physical body and subsequent energy is not there. I do not agree with this.

The marker directs attention, focus, energy. Families place flowers and gifts at the location. That attention, grief, and perhaps joy, affects the marker. People speak to it. I know I do. I've found that the dirt is plenty powerful enough to work.

In the film *Gloria,* Gloria runs from the mob with a little boy she's attempting to rescue. She constantly looks for places to hide and gather her energy. One such place is the graveyard. She tells the boy whose parents are dead to talk to his parents at one of the tombstones. He protests that that's not his family's grave. She says that they'll get the message just the same. At the end of the movie, when he believes that Gloria didn't make it, he goes to a random grave and speaks to it. Spirit knows. It's magick, not algebra. Use the memorial marking if you feel compelled.

Dirt from the Roots of Cemetery Trees

The workings of these trees are the same as for non-cemetery trees, but they are dealing with the darker aspect workings of those trees. Most trees in a cemetery exist because of deliberate planning. They carry the spirit of a tree placed in a graveyard, a heavy burden for a tree that might not have children climbing on it or even dogs marking it. It's a constant comfort to the grieving and takes on more human life than other trees. It bears the burden of being bigger than all of us, living longer than people, seeing generations bury their dead, and will one day see the stones smoothed out over time.

Cypress Tree
To cause discomfort and agony to the spirit of one's target. Whenever there is peace, a new discomfort arises, in unusual areas, unexpectedly.

Yew Tree
Many churches and churchyards once stood in a circle of yews – representing the passage from life to death and many of the older cemeteries will have a stand of yews to remind people of this passage. A yew tree growing outside of a church yard

would be the positive aspect of its energy and would be used to protect against evil.

Oak Tree

These trees live a long time, growing slowly. Often what kills them manifest as disease when limbs, too heavy for the trunk, tear off during storms leaving wounds. Dirt from these trees work on the mind, letting it to become baffled on the chore at hand and be confused. Will make a person fearful and lose all sense of strength.

Holly Tree

The realm of this tree exists in the season of the dead. Use this dirt to call upon the spirits of the dead to affect a man in a negative way. Sprinkle around an enemy's house to negatively affect them and drive them away.

Uprooted Tree

The cemetery tree has one job, and when it cannot fulfil it, it lived a life unlike other trees, away from nature or the joy of living. This dirt is dark. Any uprooted tree uprooted by nature's force symbolizes the blows of life, using dirt gathered from a tree uprooted in a graveyard, is for workings of a dark kind to bring about an uprooting in another person's life.

3-way Crossroads

When a 3-way crossroads is in the cemetery, you can use the dirt for darker aspects of Crossroads magick to cause blockages or do harm on a man's path. This is the fork in the road, the road less traveled, decisions, and angst. We stick a fork in something when it is done. It can also jam a garbage disposal. Fork in the body, known as bifurcations, can cause problems for blood flow. This type of dirt can be a very powerful addition to a sour (cursing) jar or poppet.

4-way Crossroads

Representing fulfillment, evenness, and boredom, there are many choices but also much indecision. There are four suits in tarot card decks and in playing card decks. These suits contain both good fortune and bad. When a 4-way crossroads is in the cemetery, you can use the dirt for darker aspects of Crossroads magick to block or do harm on a woman's path.

When is it Desecration?

It is said that the dead can help the living, and so graves are often visited for advice or assistance. The dead are also thought to be able to see things that the living cannot, and so they can be consulted for prophecies or warnings.

But not every graveyard is accessible to us. Yes, you can walk into almost any graveyard but that doesn't mean you should collect or honor that dirt. That ain't your dirt.

There is opportunity for deeper level connections with the dead through cultural, regional, and shared experiences. So, when collecting graveyard dirt, it is important to consider your role in the community. If you aren't an active part of that community, you ought not take anything. In blunt words, don't be a graveyard tourist and don't be taking dirt from spirit folk without a connection. A very striking example of this would be Plantation graveyards and other places enslaved folks were laid to rest. These graves should only be cared for and never taken from unless there is a profound personal connection.

Many cemeteries consider the collection of graveyard dirt to fall under desecration of the grave. You should only be taking small amounts to begin with but be certain not to alter the landscape. Avoid damaging fungi and plant life. In the rare event you find any insects within the dirt, please release them. The soil closest to older tombstones should also be avoided as the ground is often instrumental in keeping older markers upright.

Try to make your visit, even if brief, a positive one. Clean up any trash, straighten the fallen decorations, pull weeds around the chosen site, speak softly and keep any music low. Make sure to leave the site a little nicer than you found it if possible.

That being said, here are some tips for collecting graveyard dirt:

- If you don't have a familial or shared experience connection, consider the role you play in the community before taking anything.
- Don't be a graveyard tourist – only take dirt from graves that you have a connection to.
- When in doubt, ask permission from the spirit of the grave before taking anything.

Remember honor, reference, and respect. Do not take what is not yours and what you have no connection or right to. When working with graveyard dirt, it is important to be respectful. This is not play dirt. It is the final resting place of someone's loved one. Approach any graveyard with reverence and respect. Ask permission before taking any dirt. And be sure to thank the spirits when you are finished.

Useful Tools to Bring

My preference is to use a sturdy spoon rather than a spade, shovel, or garden instrument. This also stops any questions of *"Why do you have a shovel?"*, when standing in a graveyard. Most recipes only call for a pinch of graveyard dirt unless you are making Goofer Dust. For that, you will need at least a ½ cup. A small bottle is an ideal container or a handkerchief. I try to not use plastic bags unless I must (it is more environmentally conscious, and I like sea life).

The Basics

Container to put dirt in (I use a white handkerchief)

A digging tool (I use a soup spoon)

A flashlight (the one on your phone works great)

Offerings create an energetic exchange between the living and the dead reaffirming the sacred relationship that already exists.

Show Your Respect – Offer Thanks

Methods by which one acquires graveyard dirt vary vastly from practitioner to practitioner. You have to get in touch with the ancestral spirit and make a respectful request and offering. There are numerous details: who's grave, the kind of death they died, where the grave is located with respect to the cemetery gates, whether you dig from the head, the heart, or the feet, whether you leave dimes or pennies or whiskey or a combination, and where your offering is placed with respect to the grave. What you're offering may depend on the person you're taking the dirt from.

I cannot stress enough that you do not simply walk into a graveyard and take dirt from a grave at random. That is complete disrespect. You do not know who or what you are bringing home with you, and you certainly do not want to employ any individual entity that may turn against you or harm others. Know who is in the grave before you offer an exchange for that spirit's services and never simply take the dirt without proper compensation – that is stealing.

So ultimately what is the best way to go about this? Well… keep it simple, of course, when starting out! You can expand and explore more as you progress and become comfortable with gathering and working with graveyard dirt in your own practice.

I am a traditionalist at heart and feel somethings just need to be done the way it has always been done; a method where the spirits are offered a prayer, energy, coin(s), or drink, as a way of saying thanks. Every so often, the spirit is a little demanding and wants all forms of offerings. Mostly though a few soft words while kneeling next to their grave is plenty. They will let you know. I have never used graveyard dirt from a retailer or another practitioner. I passionately believe that somethings you must do yourself and collecting graveyard dirt is one of them.

Offerings

Liquids, such as alcohol (whiskey, ciders, and rum) are common, but if you are unable or unwilling to utilize alcohol, a fruit juice such as apple or grape is appropriate, or a small morsel of honey. In other traditions, tobacco leaves, burning a candle, or a stick of incense may be appropriate. Small coins or change may be placed near the grave as well.

If you are visiting the grave of a friend or relative and happened to know the person before they passed, you may consider playing their favorite song, reading a passage from their favorite book (or a book you think they would enjoy), or bringing something they were quite fond of.

Libation

The deceased's favorite drink, rum, whiskey, wine, juices, beer, etc. Either pour the entire contents onto the ground or share with the spirit and take a few sips yourself. Don't leave a container on the gravesite unless site allows it. This can be considered "altering the landscape" and the fine is $325.00, or at least that is what I was charged. I had placed a mini can of Coca-Cola on the grave as an offering, which was against the stated rules. Live, learn and read the rules!

Bread

When you offer bread, you are offering something that for the last 30,000 years, folks have likely been eating every day, and it is associated with life and divinity. Think about the presentation of the bread. Does it look homemade or is it pre-sliced? I'm not saying to go learn to make bread before interacting with a grave, but it wouldn't hurt. Try making it personal.

Instead of getting the store brand white sandwich slices, go for the natural one from the local bakery. Present the bread well, bring it in a basket, break off a piece to set on the grave and eat a little with the spirits. Breaking bread is an ancient show of hospitality and honor. It works here, too.

Cigars

A cigar is a pleasure. People don't get addicted to cigars the way they do cigarettes, but they might smoke them often. Cigars are big and take a while to enjoy. People who smoke them know that you don't inhale but taste a cigar's smoke. When you're offering cigars, you're doing something decadent, slow, luxurious. You are appealing to the dream, special occasions, celebrations, end of the day.

Coins

Pennies, nickels, dimes, quarters are coins. Shiny is important to some practitioners and to others, blessed and cleaned. Coin offerings come in certain combinations of the coins. Three pennies, 13 pennies, one of each type, only a silver dime. What does your combination add up to be? Even numbers signify balance or stagnation. Odd numbers represent change and often substantial change. The owner of the grave might want numbers that finally calm them down. They might want numbers that match their energy. They might be bored and need the chaos. Do what feels right.

Seashells

This is important in African American lore as it denotes the Middle Passage and returning to Africa for some folks. They might also be good gifts for people who loved cruises, surfing, visiting the beach.

Stones

Although originally a Jewish custom, it is now a practice embraced by all faiths. The Jewish religion uses the placement of a rock or pebble on a headstone to keep the soul of the deceased "where it belongs."

Be aware please that there is a difference between leaving stones versus rocks at a gravesite.

For thousands of years, people memorialized their loved ones by burying and stacking large rocks, also known as cairns, on top of their graves to mark the burial site and protect them from animals. Today, leaving small stones on a grave is a way of continuing this tradition to commemorate loved ones. Handpicked stones serve as an easy and small token for anyone to show they were at the cemetery to visit and honor the ones interned there.

Leaving the Graveyard

Methods for leaving the graveyard are just as varied as collecting the dirt. I have heard many creative techniques for this. The underlying theme is respect, thankfulness, gratitude and above all reverence. I will pour a little libation, give a polite nod, sometimes stop, and say a heartfelt prayer of thanks. This is about you connecting and showing respect in a way that is meaningful to you.

Ways to Leave

1. When you leave, be sure to thank the spirits and the gatekeeper, and leave some coins on the wall. Walk or drive away without looking back. Some people like to walk out backwards to prevent spirits from going with them, but it does draw attention to you. If you have included something in your thanks about not wishing to be followed, and you have been respectful, I believe this is not necessary.

2. When you leave, pour another offering at the gate, and thank the gatekeeper if possible. Return home by a different route than you came and make three stops to confuse any spirits who might try to follow you home.

3. When leaving make sure to turn three circles in front of the entrance of graveyard. Then say a bible verse or prayer aloud while walking away and not looking back. Make sure to wipe the bottoms of your shoes off before entering your home.

What About Mullein?

Mullein is an herb that can be used in magickal workings where something needs to be 'laid to rest'. It does not have the same energies or properties of graveyard dirt.

In a few contemporary pagan circles, some people, typically ones who have never studied or been a part of cultural or regional folk magick like Hoodoo, Rootwork, or Conjure, speak against using actual Graveyard Dirt. Those that speak against it tend to be of the self-proclaimed white Witch do no harm types. No judgement. Many of them have also come up with the idea that white colored items can be used as a replacement for salt in protection workings (NO! NO! NO!).

Some of these people have gone so far as to have written articles and books stating that a certain herb or mixture of herbs can take the place of actual Graveyard Dirt. This is a complete falsehood, with research and documentation to show that there are NO substitutes no matter how badly some may try to translate the recipes. When a recipe calls for Graveyard

Dirt, you need to use actual Graveyard Dirt. There is no suitable substitution for it.

I don't believe that these people are deliberately trying to deceive folks. Let's blame the current education system. Last year, I saw a meme that joked about the witches in Macbeth making a vegan potion in their cauldron. Only the brew is already mostly vegan. For instance, "eye of newt" is mustard seed. Graveyard Dirt, however, is not a euphemism for an herb.

Recipes
To Ward off Curses or Evil Spirits Around Home

We know when something isn't right in our own homes. In the movie *Practical Magick,* Dianne Wiest as Aunt Bridget says, "What's going on in this house?" after a couple of coincidences happen during the midnight margaritas ritual. Perhaps you have some bad juju on you, a run of bad luck, or your dead boyfriend you accidentally killed, resurrected, and killed again is tormenting you from beyond the grave. Bury 13 pinches of Graveyard Dirt at each of the four corners of your house.

Do you see how that isn't an even number? It's up to you whether you put one pinch at three corners and ten at the last or whether you divide them as evenly as possible. Do what feels right.

For Home Protection

A friend of mine in the deep south lives near a lady who lives on a small plantation in the middle of town. As transitional neighborhoods go, it's an interesting site next to a dental clinic where at night gunshots ring out from a few blocks down the road. Around the house is a high wall that encloses the property and keeps a perimeter open to house several large guard dogs, including an Irish Wolfhound, a mastiff, and a German Shepherd, all over 100 pounds.

Jane knows that you surround your home in order to protect it. So too dirt can protect you and your home. Walk the outdoor perimeter of your home and sprinkle a little graveyard dirt on all the corners to protect it from dark entities, unwanted spirits, and negative energy.

Another Protection Working for Home

If you need a versatile working for any earthly or spiritual reason, mix the dirt with sea salt as you state your intention. "I call on the power of graveyard dirt for protection of my home" (or whatever you're protecting). "This dirt guards the passageway between life and death, and it provides that same protection to my home."

Walk around the outside of your home and sprinkle the salt and dirt mixture in a continuous circle. If you're using this working to protect yourself or your loved one, sprinkle dirt over the person you want to protect, whispering your intention. Try sprinkling it in a continuous spiral in a certain area of the yard if you cannot walk the perimeter. Perhaps sprinkle it in the potting soil of your only houseplant in the overpriced small room that you rent for 750 dollars in the metro areas.

Another version of this protective working is to sprinkle salt and dirt mixture on a tea light or over the top of a candle as you state your intention (aloud or in your head). Light the candle and let it burn down. Once it burns down completely, your protection working has been cast. For best results, perform this protection working on the night of the full moon.

Protection from Others

Carry 13 pinches of Graveyard Dirt in a black cotton bag wrapped with a red string to protect you from negative or harmful actions of others, curses, and unwanted spirits.

To Curse Someone

Place some Graveyard Dirt upon the enemy's pathway and steps or put some in a red bag and bury it on their property. Adding the dirt to a sour jar or poppet are other well-known methods for cursing and hexing. Bring your spoon, dig down deep, past the top layer of soil. Replace the grass or stones back on top of where you removed a small bit of dirt, so no one knows what you have done.

Cause Death

If you wish to harm someone, use graveyard dirt. It is used to symbolize death to your enemy. Light a black candle symbolizing the enemy and deliberately extinguish it by turning it upside down into a saucer of graveyard dirt while stating your intention aloud. The dark moon is an excellent time to do this. Bury remains at an abandoned crossroads.

Honoring the Dead Rituals

Include graveyard dirt in rituals to honor the dead or during the season of the dead. Sprinkle some around the perimeter of your magickal circle to include the spirits of your ancestors and other chosen spirit guides in your ritual. Get your participants to bring their own dirt to throw into the sacred fire. Or bring enough dirt for all of them to do a group working for guidance and wisdom.

Communicating with the Dead

Use tarot cards, or oracle cards you are connected to, to communicate with a loved one from beyond the grave. You will need to put the graveyard dirt in a small, drawstring bag and store it with your tarot cards for a full moon cycle. During the dark moon, draw your cards and read them. If you feel like returning your cards to storage with the same dirt, do so. You might want to switch out the dirt with someone else's dirt to see if it changes the vibe of the readings.

Making a Major Life Decision

Leave some graveyard dirt at a crossroads when trying to decide between two paths in life. Assign one path to symbolize one option, and one path to symbolize the other. An example for this would be: the westward path represents a decision based on your emotion or heart, or an Eastward path to represent an intellectual decision. Once you decide which way to go, walk down your chosen path and sprinkle graveyard dirt to "seal off" second-guesses or regrets. Walk away and do not look back.

In the Garden

During the fall season, sprinkle graveyard dirt in your home garden to honor the cycle of life and encourage the dead to "come back" in the form of your crop, a lovely representation of reincarnation.

All Protection Workings/Spells

Add graveyard dirt to protection sachets, bags, and workings to provide an extra punch.

New Beginnings

Death gives way to new life. If you're starting a new chapter in your life (a new job, for example, or a new living situation), select an object that represents your past circumstances and bury it with the graveyard dirt to put your old situation behind you for good with a very powerful ritual of "closure."

Ending a Romantic Relationship

Sometimes, ex-lovers or partners melodramatically declare "You're dead to me!" and storm off in an almost award-winning fashion. A quieter, more private declaration is usually much more sincere and far more effective. Gather your mementos of the relationship, and photos you may have. Build a fire in a safe and sane matter. Take the objects and put in the fire, burning them completely. Say or shout words of your personal closure. Maybe something like "this is over", "you are dead to me" or "never to return". When ready extinguish it with graveyard dirt. Be aware this working requires a full handful of dirt or more. It is quite effective when done with full energic commitment. Also, a great night to invite friends over to help with.

Mourning
Leave a small jar of graveyard dirt from a recently deceased loved one on the altar during your mourning period to honor their memory and keep them close to the heart. Place a bit of dirt in a token (bag, charm holder, be creative) and wear or keep with you for comfort and connection.

Protection from a Loved One Beyond the Grave
Fill a red bag with a small amount of dirt taken from the grave site of a loved one. Add one flower from the funeral and a pebble from the graveyard. Anoint the bag with drop of the deceased's favorite perfume or cologne. This bag can be placed on your altar or worn or carried with you as a protective charm.

Binding
Graveyard Dirt can bind two people together. To perform this binding working, collect dirt from a graveyard and choose the person you desire to bind yourself to. Write your name and that other person's name on a piece of paper and draw one circle around both of your names.

Fold up the paper and put it in a bag. Sprinkle the graveyard dirt into the bag and state your intention. Something like, "With this graveyard dirt, I bind (person's name) and myself together until death do us part."

This working should be used with extreme caution because it is common for folks to regret binding themselves to others because feelings sometimes change. This working is powerful, and it should not be taken lightly. If you perform this working and need to reverse it for any reason, you can burn the paper, the dirt, and the bag in a safe and sane matter. Scatter the ashes in a flowing body of water like a river or fast-moving stream.

Goofer Dust

References to this dark concoction abound in southern lore and were sung about by Bluesman, Cripple Clarence Lofton, in his song, *I Don't Know. (1938)*

> *Gettin' sick and tired of the way you do*
> *'Time Mama I'm gonna poison you*
> *Sprinkle goofer dust around your hed*
> *Wake up some mornin' find your own self dead*

The word "Goofer" in Goofer Dust is a bastardization of the Kikongo word "Kufwa" = meaning "To Die." In effect, Goofer Dust is "magickal killing powder" or poison. It is perhaps the strongest black magick powder found in the practice of American folk magick. There are innumerable recipes among magickal practitioners for Goofer Dust, but all have one thing in common: dirt from a grave.

Occasionally the term Goofer Dust is used as a synonym for graveyard dirt but graveyard dirt is but one ingredient in a recipe for Goofer Dust. One utilizes Goofer Dust in only the most destructive of workings: to curse, hex, trick, poison, or kill an enemy.

When I was beginning a magickal group in a new home, I used just a tad of Goofer Dust mixed with a few other magickal ingredients on a prospective member to confirm whether their intentions were good or bad. I brought a box of magickal items and capes for the new practitioners to try. One cloak, though, I specified for one person.

It was on that cloak that I sprinkled my goofer dust mixture. I did a working in a way that if the individual was genuine then everything would be fine, and if their reasons for coming were nefarious, then they would leave. I never saw them again. Goofer dust caused this person to leave because they did not have good or pure intentions.

Goofer Dust is a handy tool for some magickal practitioners. It is often found in occult stores or online in pre-packaged bottles or packets. The only problem is that many of the types of so called Goofer Dusts sold online are not true Goofer Dusts. They are commercially created fakes, which are passed off to unknowing buyers as the real thing, when they are anything but the real thing.

Some people and groups sell a variety of crushed herbs, others use herbs mixed with colored sawdust, while some others are selling tinted talcum powders and claiming that they have magickal properties. Liars gleefully abound where money is concerned.

A Hoodoo practitioner taught me in a workshop that the presence of iron filings within the formula points to the true origins of how this powder was originally prepared and empowered. While iron has been associated with both good workings such as repelling evil, and in negative aspects such as being referred to as the "Bones of Set" in Egyptian folklore, it has one interesting use that makes sense involving goofer dust.

Iron bars are used around cemeteries to keep the spirits of the dead within its confines. The same material could be used to keep spiritual energy connected to the powder as well. A spiritual energy that would be attached to the powder both from the graveyard dirt, and from the iron used within the powder as a base for a particular spirit to work through. Goofer Dust when made in the traditional way is far more necromantic than it is given credit for today. It is *conjure* in the purest sense of the word.

The connection between iron and the human body exists in blood. Perhaps iron shaving serves better than bloodletting to make goofer dust. It's the same element after all.

The actual recipe for goofer dust differs from practitioner to practitioner. Traditionally this powder is put wherever the person must walk through it. It's usually more effective if the person is barefoot or wears sandals or open style shoe. It can also be added to a scented talcum powder and used to dust the inside of shoes. It causes severe discomfort and is used to drive people away or worse if you desire.

True Goofer Dust is best made by the person who plans to use it. It may also be purchased from well-known or respected practitioner that can be trusted to be honest about the ingredients. This is necessary in order to insure it is the real thing and as potent as necessary for the types of controlling and/or baneful magick that the concoction is used for.

Once formulated the powder is traditionally utilized by sprinkling in the path of the enemy. Usually this is done by sprinkling the power while walking backward in an odd number of steps, while praying for the intended magickal effect.

One may also snuff a curse candle (such as a Black Skull) with Goofer Dust. Keep a bowl of Goofer Dust in the ritual area and snuff the candle upside-down in the bowl to intensify the curse.

To cause an enemy to waste away, collect dirt from the enemy's footprint, mix it with Goofer Dust, and seal the mixture in a bottle. Seal the bottle with a black candle, anointed with Black Arts Oil. Then hide the bottle in a hollow of a tree (for hope of eventual reversal of the spell) or cast it in the river (for a permanent working).

So, if you want to get your spouse/ boyfriend/girlfriend or freeloader, out of the house, put Goofer Dust where he or she must walk through it. If you find that your significant other has been cheating on you in the worse possible way, use Goofer Dust. Make sure you don't get into the stuff yourself, carefully sprinkle a small amount in and around their shoes. Sprinkle a little under their pillow, or on their mattress but under the bottom sheet. If you use this method, do not share their bed.

When the target steps on the goofer dust it is believed to magickally "poison them through their feet". More inventive practitioners may find other uses for goofer dust, such as to sprinkle it on the target's mattress, laundry, or in their shoes, or on the edge of a cloak. Other hidden forms of deployment include placing the goofer dust in a mojo bag or bottle which is secretly hidden in the home of the target or buried on their property, preferably near to where the target will walk.

Besides the laying of some Goofer Dust in your enemy's tracks to poison them through their feet, you can dress candles with Goofer Dust to curse your enemies and toss the remains in the graveyard, so they'll end up there. Some folks will sprinkle Goofer Dust into food to serve to their enemy to destroy their health and leave them languishing on the floor wailing in anguish. Because graveyard dirt is used, sulfur might be present; it's possible that the meal would taste terrible and would not be palatable.

Remember to cleanse yourself with an Uncrossing Herbal Bath after using Goofer Dust to take the powerful evil of this curse off you. I cannot stress enough that this is horrible stuff. Please handle with care, keep away from eyes and mouth (and children and pets), do not burn as incense, and take a spiritual cleansing bath after you use.

If you or anyone unintended falls ill, sprinkle salt in the corners of your house, and commence sweeping and washing. Be sure to ritually cleanse the unintended victim, preferably in a magickal bath. Modern medicine will have no effect on being goofered. If you or a loved one is goofered go immediately to someone VERY knowledgeable in American folk magick; Hoodoo, Root work, Conjure, etc. to remove the curse.

To thoroughly cleanse your home, scrub the floor with fresh clean water and your urine, or urine from a child. You can also use other types of floor washing waters; Holy Herb Wash or 7 Holy Herbs floor wash, which can be purchased from a few folk magick dealers online. When you are done with it, discard the water off your property, throw it at a crossroads, if possible, away from your home and never carry this water out the front door of your home.

Folks who have been successfully cursed with goofer dust are referred to as being "goofered", and sometimes the term goofered is used as a synonym for being cursed or poisoned. People who have been goofered will begin to experience extreme bad luck, dangerous health complaints, insanity, and even death if the proper magickal procedures are not performed to remove the cursed condition.

Though normally deployed in dark magick workings for revenge, goofer dust is sometimes used in love workings designed to make a specific person love deeply and madly whoever the practitioner desires. But it is no love working, more like love me or die. Such workings also fall under the category of malevolent magick as they interfere with the free will of the intended person.

These types of workings are designed to produce pain and suffering in the target to force them to submit. If by chance the target does not submit, then they may eventually die if the curse/love working is not removed with the proper counter-rituals.

Goofer Recipes

Warning! When making or handling goofer dust wear medical disposable gloves and a mask to protect yourself.

Classic Goofer Dust Recipe

This recipe dates to the turn of the 20th century (early 1900's). They did not write all of their details down a lot of times for fear someone would steal the recipe. Also, the use of code names was quite common with hiding names of actual ingredients. It is supposed that this pied information (purposeful misinformation or misdirection) is what created the myth of mullein substitution for graveyard dirt.

Handful of Graveyard Dirt
Equal handful of Sulfur
Dried and ground venomous snakeskin
Small amount of Iron fillings from an old railroad spike

Modern Goofer Dust Recipe

Here you will see the addition of the spirit of the root being incorporated into the recipe. Old school magickal practitioners do not agree with the additions of herbs, flowers, etc. while many modern practitioners will say "why not?". Old school maintains that the recipe's effect is "and you shall die" and that herbs and flowers theoretically make it pretty and less effective. They also believe that Goofer dust should never smell good. The modern practitioners feel that the additions intensify and aid in the recipe. Elevation or watering down? That is a personal decision that you must make. Ultimately do what feels right for you and your situation.

You will need:

1/4 cup Sulfur aka "Brimstone"

1/4 cup Salt (old school style was to use non-iodized sea salt in the 1930's and 40's. Later on, Black salt or Witches' Salt was used when the European influence came in.)

1 tablespoon Either the skin or head of a venomous snake, dried and ground

1 tablespoon Black pepper finely ground

3/4's cup Graveyard Dirt preferable from the grave of a murderer, ideally collected after midnight

1 tablespoon hot Red or Cayanne pepper

A pinch of magnetic sand

Once you have all the ingredients, you need to grind them together and store them in an airtight container. Mark it clearly as Goofer Dust. Just as with War Water and a few other dangerous items, Goofer Dust is one of those magickal items that you certainly do not want to use by mistake!

Be certain to cleanse the work area thoroughly after creating the Goofer Dust. Clean any tools used, the altar and/or preparation areas, even the outside of the container to make certain it is all contained where it should be for your own safety.

Wipe the outside of the container with a damp paper towel making sure to dispose of quickly and safely, dispose of mask and gloves, and wash any clothing that you were wearing. Completely clean the area and wash all utensils that you were using a fresh set of disposable gloves. Mark outside of container as "POISON" and store away from children, pets, and curious eyes.

Possible Herbal Additions:

Cayanne Pepper – hurry along

Thistle – crossing and hexing enemies

Hemlock – paralyzing negative situations

Hydrangea – binding enemies

Knotweed – binding, controlling the magick of others and cursing enemies

Morning Glory – binding enemies

Nettle – returning a hex to another

Paprika – crossing an enemy

Solomon's Seal Root – binding the magick and spell work of others

Wormwood – crossing and hexing enemies

Yerba Mate – ending relationships

Any herbs of success and completion

Some magickal practitioners will choose never to use Goofer Dust, but for those who do choose to use it, it is a powerful tool and handy to have around.

Another Goofer Ritual

Take personal items of the person you want goofered, such as hair, a tissue, some tiny personal item they won't miss. Put the item into a jar and add goofer dust. Seal the jar securely and shake it to mix thoroughly. Then go to a stagnate water source, preferably swamp like. You can use any natural water source available (lake, stream, ocean) if the swamp isn't an option. When you are ready to throw it in the water, pierce a hole in the top of the lid, it doesn't have to be big. Now throw it into the water and walk away not looking back. As it sinks, the person will begin wasting away.

Alternative Goofer Ritual

This powder can be used in other rituals to rid yourself of any unwanted person. An alternative to using it the traditional way is to place some Goofer Dust in a cardboard box like a shoe box or something smaller like one of those jewelry gift boxes, then place a picture of your target alone in the box, if you have anything like hair or a personal item add that to the box and bury it but bury it far away from your own home, where the cardboard box will rot.

How to Tell if You've Been Goofered

Traditionally it is believed that if a person wears on an ankle bracelet or chain with a real silver dime charm (before 1964) it will tell you if you have been goofered. The dime first needs to be cleaned with a little baking soda and water before it's attached to the ankle bracelet. If the dime gets very tarnished, then that person has been goofered and needs to do cleansing ritual baths and other rituals. Another way is to have the dime taped to the bottom of your foot overnight and if it tarnishes that is a sign you have been goofered. Another way to tell is sudden changes in health and behavior, which might show up later if nothing is done.

Reversing a Goofer Spell

The rituals performed to counteract goofering include spiritual baths, the burning of candles and incense, and cleansing or "uncrossing" rituals of the afflicted individual and of the home and property. After these rituals have been completed, it is often followed with rituals of protection from further attack or to reverse the curse back to the sender.

The method for reversing a goofer working can vary, but the first thing immediately is to wash the bottoms of your feet, scrub them hard with salt and vinegar for several minutes. Then take a shower and wash yourself with either an unscented soap such as Ivory, an oatmeal-based soap or a Ruda soap.

Wash yourself from the top of your head to between the toes of your feet and the bottoms of your feet. Place a muslin bag filled with Hyssop herb on the floor of the shower and allow the essence of the herb to fill the area. Again, wash all over you while saying aloud three times "Cleanse me with Hyssop O Lord, that I maybe as pure as the whitest snow."

Then wash or dry clean all your clothes and underwear, if you have a lot do it a load at a time, be sure to wear gloves, make sure all your shoes are cleaned from the inside and out, wash your bed linens, vacuum, and meticulously dust your house. Damp down your dust mop with a lemon furniture polish spray or a citrus oil blend. You need to throw your dust mop heads away, so using disposable ones is preferable. Wear a hospital type filter mask and disposable gloves while doing all this.

Still wearing gloves and a mask, sweep your front and back porch, steps and pathway with an old broom and a disposable dustpan, any dust you find put into a paper bag and firmly seal it. Then put the broom, dustpan, and the bag into a large garbage bag, along with the gloves and mask that you used, take it to the dump or garbage disposal facility.

Follow up with other spiritual baths, uncrossing rituals, and candles both on the person and the property. You may consider trying to determine who might have "goofered" the person and do a reversing ritual.

Chapter 5

Middleton Journals

Who would have thought that an Episcopalian minister would write one of the greatest magick books of American folk magick history? That happened. Henry Middleton Hyatt traveled from the deep south to New York, collecting observations, interviews, and ultimately, magickal workings. Most, if not all, of the workings in this collection come from black folk. This presents a problem. How forthcoming and how authentic is the information given if the interviewee might not have felt so free giving it.

While there is no evidence that Henry Middleton Hyatt intimidated anyone, after all he was born in the same town that Abraham Lincoln represented in state legislature, one wonders if stereotypes or even the novelty of a white guy interviewing a different race of people during a time of segregation can yield the best results.

The interview might have been 100% positive for all parties involved, but haven't you ever embellished a story to impress a new person? Have you ever deliberately downplayed a story that your friends forced you to retell for the umpteenth time? All of these considerations must be made when we read these volumes.

While all the aforementioned currents existed, we cannot discount the invaluable insight these works gives into a magickal practice that previously had only been discussed in whispered corners. For years I poured over entries and have found supporting evidence for many of the methods revealed in these volumes. These journals need to be embraced with honesty and understanding and above all with reverence for the folks who shared their stories.

I have gone through the *Middleton Journals*, and for those who are not familiar with the Hyatt books; *Hoodoo - Conjuration Witchcraft - Rootwork*, is a 5-volume, 4766 page collection of folkloric material gathered by Hyatt in Alabama, Arkansas, Florida, Georgia, Illinois, Louisiana, Maryland, Mississippi, North Carolina, South Carolina, Tennessee, and Virginia between 1936 and 1940. The *Middleton* collection consists of 13,458 separate magick workings and folkloric beliefs, in addition to lengthy interviews with professional root doctors, conjures, and hoodoos", looking for glimpses into our collected past and finding mutual experiences and solutions.

Based on my experience working with a Haitian Vodou Priest for over almost thirty years and whose shop brought in root workers, conjurers, hoodoo folk from all over the low country of South Carolina, North Carolina, and Georgia, I can see insights, inking lings, and intuition about the workings in these journals. Some seem ready to use. Some seem like diversions, some lies, some way too embellished to be believable, and some truth. Such is life.

I leave it to you the reader, magickal practitioner, or the curious to decide how this information is used in your own life. At the very least these stories are a link to our magickal past that need to be shared with the full disclosure of how the knowledge was obtained. Below you will read a small sampling of the actual entries as they were originally collected in the 1930's with vernacular variants in speech. Meaning Hyatt recorded the regional dialects, and the way folks were actually speaking.

Time Correspondences for Obtaining Graveyard Dirt

9 o'clock at night – north side of the graveyard
Go to the graveyard at nine o'clock at night and get some dirt out of a grave on the north side of the cemetery. And carry it to a woman's house that has a husband, and you want that husband.

You get some of your friends to take that dirt there. And if she can become friendly with the woman in that house and get a chance to sprinkle it around their bed and in the house, so she will have to walk over it, this woman, this man's wife will dwindle away and die. Then you have the opportunity to get with this man. [Memphis, Tenn.]

Midnight
People say that if you have been having tough luck and haven't had much success, go to the graveyard at midnight and get some graveyard dirt and put it in little sacks or bags (tiny ones) and wear them around your waist. And from time to time you will be more successful that if you didn't do this. [St. Petersburg, Fla.]

Midnight – no moon shining
At twelve o'clock at night you get graveyard dirt. That's mostly for harming, that for nothing good. You go there at midnight but when the moon is not shining. You go there on a dark night. And you take the graveyard dirt. If you just want a person to have bad luck, you just throw the dirt at the person – strictly without anything else. They will never be successful in any undertaking that they do. [New Orleans, La.]

New moon – innocent's grave
If she wants to run around on you. You go to the graveyard on a new moon and get some dirt off an innocent's grave, take sulfur and table salt. And when she leaves the house, you go into her room and throw it in the room, and as she goes out the door you throw it in the name of the father, the son, and the holy ghost, and go on. Just like she comes in at night, you know, like she is going out at night, and she doesn't want them to be out looking for her. Well, she gets it fresh. She goes there on a new moon. (She does this, so they won't bother her while she goes out at night?) Go anywhere she wants. [Fayetteville, N. Car.]

One o'clock in morning

I heard that if you go to the graveyard, go there at one o'clock in the morning and get graveyard dirt. Get the graveyard dirt and bring it back and then sprinkle it on people's porch, anyone's porch to make them move. [Memphis, Tenn.]

4 o'clock in the morning

Go to the graveyard around four in the morning and buy a penny worth of graveyard dirt. And come back and sprinkle it around the house, all around and sweep off they do step behind them. That will move them. Sweeping graveyard dirt is both an uncommon and dangerous rite. The woman here that wants to rid herself of an unwelcome roomer or friend, sprinkles graveyard dirt about the house outside, leaving herself a dirties entry. Coming indoors she closes the dirt less entry, the doorstep, with graveyard dirt. She is a prisoner in her own home. But, as soon as he walks over the dirt, entering or leaving, she sweeps it away. The spirit in graveyard dirt, not liking to be swept by the dirty broom, flees back to the graveyard; the man, having crossed the dirt, must go away forever; and the woman, now immune from the graveyard-dirt spirit, is free – for another roomer or friend. (How much dirt do you get from the graveyard?) Penny's worth. (How much would that be?) That would be two ounces. [Wilson, N. Car.]

Before sunrise – throw in direction victim lives – bible

They can do most anything with it, such as hurting a person. You can take graveyard dirt and you can cause a person to, if you don't want them to stay there, you can cause them to move to another place. But you must go to the graveyard soon, before morning, before the rising of the sun, get the dirt and cast it in the direction the person lives. If you cast it in the direction the person lives and read a portion from the Bible, they will move immediately. (Did you say portion or any particular portion?) Just any portion of the Bible, doesn't matter, just any portion to drive most anyone away with graveyard dirt. [Vicksburg, Miss.]

Before sunrise – dirt from the heart

There are a lot of people who say if you go to the graveyard, say, just before morning and dig down right about the heart of a person, right about the breast of a person, dig down way deep into the grave and get the graveyard dirt, no doubt, and put it in your shoes or wrap it in a rag, and place in your pocket, this is good for luck in gambling. [St. Petersburg, Fla.]

Full moon – dirt from a fresh grave to bring in customers

You use the dead man, and the way they mix it, you mix the dirt taken from a fresh grave on a full moon. Mix the Sulphur and red pepper and bury it under the foot of a step, and it brings in customers/ persons. [Sumter, S. Car]

Graveyard Dirt and salt in bottle – sprinkle under steps

They get the dirt out of a graveyard, and they stop it up in a bottle and they will come to your house. If they don't like you, they will come to your house with the graveyard dirt. Mix it with a little salt and sprinkle it under the steps. Then they stop the other one tight and bury it. But you're not supposed to be home when they do that, and anytime you go back to that house where your spirit has gone. That drives your spirit away. You'd go to the house, but you can't stay. [Jacksonville, Fla.]

Graveyard dust under bed

Get a little graveyard dirt and put on a person, and when you put it on them – get a little graveyard dirt and carry it, tie it up real tight and put it up under the pillow and let them sleep on it at night. And if he's got a wife and his wife wanted to go out, she would put it up under there and let him to go sleep. If he's got whiskey in him or anything – anything at all like whiskey on him she can go on off and stay just long as she wants. And when she comes back, she'll pull it out and he wakes up. (That's to keep him asleep while she is gone.) [Florence, S. Car.]

Graveyard Dirt sprinkle on hair or head

Take graveyard dust...sprinkle it...over your hair...that will make you sleep. [Vicksburg, Mis.]

Person's grave-type correspondences

Just as the times & phases when dirt is taken plays a significant role in its' usage, so does the various types of graves it is taken from. The dirt is thought to work special magick in accordance with the type of person who inhabits the grave as you will see in the following examples.

Baby's grave

If you want two women to get along, wanted them to live in the same house together. Well, you go to the graveyard where a baby is buried, run your hand down there and get some dirt from the head. Come home and sprinkle it around the house nine morning in a row and that will make peace in the house. (What do you mean have two women in the house and have them get along?) If you have two of them and you just want them to get along. If they stay in separate houses, it will be all right, but you have to sprinkle it in both houses. (I see) You could put them in the house together is you use the dirt. (You mean the two women?) Yes. [Vicksburg, Miss.]

Well, if you want a job of any kind, you get a dirt dauber and go to a baby's grave in the cemetery and reach your hand down in the same direction. And if you want a job anywhere, you mix the same dirt, the dirt dauber nest with the other dirt. And sprinkle in in front of the place and around the office where the boss has got to go in, and just say, "Little baby, in the name of the father, son and the holy ghost, give me my job back". And they give it to you. [Brunswick, Ga.]

I heard that you can take a dirt dauber nest and some graveyard dirt from a little baby. If you know it and mix it together and put it somewhere, about the bed or in the corner of some hidden place, and the baby terrify you and cry so – the spirit will – that will leave out of the room. (That is to make you move) [Sumter, S. Car.]

Catholic's grave

You go to the Catholic Graveyard and reach down in there, dig down in there and get some grave off the breast. *(A woman's?)* It doesn't make any difference, but it has to be a Catholic's grave where you get the dirt. Take that dirt and you get some gourd seeds *(green seeds)* and you get some red pepper and take nine grains out of the red pepper. Then you get a good bit of the mixture and go to the fork in the road and sprinkle a little bit there. Do this for 3 nights and on the third night call out the party's name and they will return. [Mobile, Ala.]

Child's grave

They say if you have an enemy around and you want to drive them away from you, go to the graveyard, to the grave of a child. You run your hand down there to the elbow and grab a handful of dirt. You go to the persons house, you can go all around [circumambulate] his house, and scatter dirt [also] on his step. You will cause a fuss in their house, and they will be gone. [Wilmington N. Car.]

A spiritual man (usually a person working largely with spirits)

Can sit home and wait for the coming of the good man's spirit and use it for curing. If the sick or hoodooed person is not too far gone. [Savannah, Ga.]

Sinner's grave

Go to the graveyard and carry 3 pennies in your hand, reach down, if it is the grave of a sinner, if it is someone who didn't have a religion. You dig a little hole and leave the 3 pennies and take some dirt with you. *(Then you use the dirt?)* You can take the graveyard dust and sprinkle it around your home, and this will break up you and your

husband. It will cause confusion in your home, but it has to be from a
sinner's grave [New Orleans, La.]

You can also sprinkle it in the corners of one room where people
penetrate, like the front room and their minds will be stirred up, and
they will have to leave. (They couldn't stay there.) [Brunswick, Ga.]

Woman's grave to bring back a woman

Dirt from woman's grave – scrape a little from top, take home. light
2 black candles – set under be where she [woman who left home] has
been sleeping – put graveyard dust and sprinkle a ring [of it] around
candles – and a piece of her clothes and lay where she sleeps – turn
mattress up and lay the clothes on springs on a paper. Take Bible and
say prayers and read Bible – when candles go out, she'll come home.
[Memphis, Tenn.]

End Notes

The Principles of Magick

This is the basis of all modern magick. No matter what system of magick you are drawn to; Traditional, Folk, Ceremonial, Christian Mysticism, they all operate within the Four Powers of the Magus for obtaining successful results.

The Four Powers of the Magus

- To Know
- To Dare
- To Will
- To Keep Silent

To Know

Knowledge is the cornerstone to all activities in the magickal realms. Don't just rely on one source. Instead gather as much information as you can on the subject. Even contrary or conflicting views will give you more insight. Always look to discover new ideas, not confirm beliefs held. Keep open to new ideas, ways, methods, and you will always be growing.

To Dare

Action with knowledge is to dare. What stops most folks is *belief of self*. Three words that many spend a lifetime never achieving. You must dare to put the knowledge you have learned to use.

To Will

To have no doubt. Never speaking of "if it works" only "when it works". When the word "if" is used it creates a place for doubt to grow and ultimately failure is the result. When we do a working, we always want to speak as if it has already successfully happened.

To Keep Silent

When we let others know what we are doing we are giving them an opportunity to influence our work. Maybe that is a good thing or just maybe that is a bad thing. Why take the chance?

References

Cemeteries & Gravemarkers, Voices of American Culture; Richard E. Myer, UMI Research Press, 1989

Honoring Your Ancestors; Mallorie Vaudoise, Llewellyn Publications, 2019

Love Cemetery, Unburying the Secret History of Slaves; China Gallard, Harper One, 2008

Grave Exclamations: An Analysis of Tombstones and Their Use as Narrative of Self; Lacey Jae Ritter, Thesis, Minnesota State University – Mankato 2012

Beautiful Death; Art of the Cemetery; David Robinson, Penguin Books, 1996

Legends and Lore of South Carolina; Sherman Carmichael, The History Press, 2012

Magical House Protection, The Archaeology of Counter-Witchcraft; Brain Hoggard, Berghahn Press, 2019

New World Witchery, A Trove of North American Folk Magic; Cory Hutcheson, Llewellyn Publications, 2022

Parabola, The Magazine of Myth and Tradition, *Crossroads*; Editor - D.M. Dooling, August 1993

The Sanctified Church; Zora Neale Hurston, De Capo Press, 1998

Go Tell My Horse; Zora Neale Hurston, Amistad, 2008

Of Mules and Men; Zora Neale Hurston, Amistad, 2008.

Book of Legendary Spells; Elbee Wright, Marlar Publishing, 1968

Rest In Peace, A History of American Cemeteries; Meg Greene, Twenty First Century Books, 2008

The American Resting Place; Marilyn Yalom, Houghton Mifflin Company, 2008

Santeria: Candles, Herbs, Incense, Oils; C. Montenegro, Original Publications, 1998

Southern Cunning; Aaron Oberon, Moon Books, 2019

Crossroads Witchcraft; The Ingredients; Taren S, Independently Published, 2020

God, Dr. Buzzard and the Bolito Man; Cornelia Walker Bailey, Anchor Books, 2001

The Conjure Stories; Charles W. Chestnutt, W. W. Norton & Co., 2012

Blue Roots, African American Folk Magic of the Gullah People; Roger Pinckney, Sandlapper Publishing, 2003

Lowcountry Voodoo; Terrance Zepke, Pineapple Press, 2009

Lowcountry Voodoo, A-Z; Carole Marsh Longmeyer, Gallopade International, 2016

Digging Up the Dead; Michael Kammen, University of Chicago, 2010

The Cemetery Book, Graveyards, Catacombs and Other Travel Haunts around the World; Tom Weil, Hippocrene Books, 1992

The Supernatural, Spirits and Spirit Worlds; Roy Stemman, Danbury Press, 1975

The Victorian Book of the Dead; Chris Woodard, Kestrel Publications, 2014

Widow's Weeds and Weeping Veils; Bernadette Loeffel-Atkins, Gettysburg Publishing, 2012

The Devil's Garden; Edward R. Ricciuti, Walker & Co., 1978

British Folktales; Katherine Briggs, Pantheon Books, 1970

A Treasury of American Superstition; Claudia De Lys, Philosophical Books, 1948

The Meaning of Trees; Fred Hageneder, Chronicle Books, 2005

Irish Wild Plants - Myths, Legends, and Folklore; Nial Mac Coitir, The Collins Press, 2008

The Secret Lore of Plants and Flowers; Eric Maple, Robert Hale Press, 1980

Mojo Workin'; The African American Hoodoo System; Katrina Hazzard-Donald, University of Illinois Press, 2013

Being Dead Is No Excuse; Gayden Metcalfe & Charlotte Hays, Hachette Books, 2015

When Your Animal Dies; Sylvia Barbanell, Spiritual Truth Press, 1940

Who Will Save Your Soul; Jewel, https://www.youtube.com/watch?v=x7buR2g4nqs

Recommended Reading List

Anything by Zora Neale Thruston
New World Witchery; Cory Hutcheson
Mojo Workin'; The African American Hoodoo System; Katrina Hazzard-Donald
Honoring Your Ancestors; Mallorie Vaudoise
A Treasury of American Superstition; Claudia De Lys
God, Dr. Buzzard, and the Bolito Man; Cornelia Walker Bailey
Crossroads of Conjure; Katrina Rasbold
Drawing Down the Spirits; Kenaz Filan & Raven Kaldera

You may also like...

Hoodoo in the Psalms - God's Magick
by Taren S

*Magickal workings found in the Psalms, developed over a
millennium for the modern conjurer to use today.*

While addressing the box many of us see the Christian Psalms
in, and embracing both the Old Religion of the Pagans and the
Judeo-Christian roots of the Psalms and how they are used
in Hoodoo, Taren S presents a thorough system of magick in
the tradition of the practical occult spells books and formulas
many of us cut our teeth on. Christopher Penczak, author of
The Casting of Spells and *The Inner Temple of Witchcraft*

978-1-78904-206-1 (Paperback)
978-1-78904-207-8 (e-book)

MOON BOOKS
PAGANISM & SHAMANISM

What is Paganism? A religion, a spirituality, an alternative belief system, nature worship? You can find support for all these definitions (and many more) in dictionaries, encyclopaedias, and text books of religion, but subscribe to any one and the truth will evade you. Above all, Paganism is a creative pursuit, an encounter with reality, an exploration of meaning and an expression of the soul. Druids, Heathens, Wiccans and others, all contribute their insights and literary riches to the Pagan tradition. Moon Books invites you to begin or to deepen your own encounter, right here, right now.

If you have enjoyed this book, why not tell other readers by posting a review on your preferred book site.

Bestsellers from Moon Books

Keeping Her Keys
An Introduction to Hekate's Modern Witchcraft
Cyndi Brannen
*Blending Hekate, witchcraft and personal development together
to create a powerful new magickal perspective.*
Paperback: 978-1-78904-075-3 ebook 978-1-78904-076-0

Journey to the Dark Goddess
How to Return to Your Soul
Jane Meredith
*Discover the powerful secrets of the Dark Goddess and transform
your depression, grief and pain into healing and integration.*
Paperback: 978-1-84694-677-6 ebook: 978-1-78099-223-5

Shamanic Reiki
Expanded Ways of Working with Universal Life Force Energy
Llyn Roberts, Robert Levy
*Shamanism and Reiki are each powerful ways of healing; together,
their power multiplies. Shamanic Reiki introduces techniques to
help healers and Reiki practitioners tap ancient healing wisdom.*
Paperback: 978-1-84694-037-8 ebook: 978-1-84694-650-9

Southern Cunning
Folkloric Witchcraft in the American South
Aaron Oberon
*Modern witchcraft with a Southern flair, this book is a journey
through the folklore of the American South and a look at the power
these stories hold for modern witches.*
Paperback: 978-1-78904-196-5 ebook: 978-1-78904-197-2

Readers of ebooks can buy or view any of these bestsellers by clicking on the live link in the title. Most titles are published in paperback and as an ebook. Paperbacks are available in traditional bookshops. Both print and ebook formats are available online.

Find more titles and sign up to our readers' newsletter
http://www.johnhuntpublishing.com/paganism

Follow us on Facebook
https://www.facebook.com/MoonBooks

Follow us on Instagram
https://www.instagram.com/moonbooksjhp/

Follow us on Twitter
https://twitter.com/MoonBooksJHP

Follow us on TikTok
https://www.tiktok.com/@moonbooksjhp